The Edge of Adventure

Long before *recovery* became a household word, Keith Miller was holding forth a bold message of spiritual renewal through his books and seminars. Now his popular volume *The Edge of Adventure* has been updated for the 1990s.

In *The Edge of Adventure,* Bruce Larson joins Keith Miller in an adventure that leads to total commitment to God—and real faith. Through their writings and personal observations these two close friends in Christ creatively explore what it means to live truly with and for him.

This evangelical classic is written in a compelling and honest spirit; highly readable, practical, and motivating. It meets a vital need of all Christians—those new in the faith, those who want to continue to mature and explore spiritual growth, and those who are dissatisfied in their personal relationship with Jesus Christ. And it offers new hope and a sense of direction for living the Christian life to its fullest.

REVISED EDITION

THE
EDGE
OF
ADVENTURE

KEITH MILLER
AND
BRUCE LARSON

Fleming H. Revell Company
Tarrytown, New York

Library of Congress Cataloging-in-Publication Data

Miller, Keith.
The edge of adventure / Keith Miller and Bruce Larson.
p.   c.m.
Includes bibliographical references.
ISBN 0-8007-5414-X
1. Christian Life—1960–   2. Miller, Keith.   3. Larson, Bruce.
4. Christian biography—United States.   I. Larson, Bruce.
II. Title.
BV4501.2.M4789   1991
248′.092′2—dc20
[B]   91-35604
CIP

Copyright © 1974, 1991 by Keith Miller and Bruce Larson
Published by the Fleming H. Revell Company
Tarrytown, New York 10591
Printed in the United States of America

CONTENTS

INTRODUCTION

❖ HAVE YOU EVER WONDERED WHAT WOULD happen to you if you *really* tried to commit your whole life to God?—to give him the keys to your future and then set out to find and do his will in the rest of your life?

In very different ways, and coming from quite different backgrounds, we (Bruce Larson and Keith Miller) began such an adventure several years ago—having no idea where it would take us or what kinds of partings and new beginnings the adventure would involve. Would God send us overseas? Or merely give us new perspectives to guide us where we lived? We began to try to determine, each in his own way (and without knowing the other), what it might mean to try to live with Christ as both guide and model in our attempts to relate to God and the people around us. We found ourselves confronted by the need to examine our roles as husbands and fathers, at work, in considering changes in our vocational lives, and in facing the fears, moral failures, and those "disappearances" of our faith which come along periodically in our lives.

One of us is ordained and one a layman. We have both been appalled at our lack of basic honesty, at our fear of failing and having our inadequacies discovered. We have been disappointed at our recurring attempts to replace Christ as the center of our separate worlds, trying to impress people and even each other with our importance and accomplishments. This has been especially painful since we both love God very much and like to think of ourselves as humble men of integrity.

It is only natural that two men with such similar problems and aspirations might meet (as we did in 1962) and become close friends.

Each of us has discovered that the best way he's found to learn and teach about the Christian life is to accept the hypothesis that God really was "in Christ reconciling the world to himself" and that it *is* possible to communicate with him through prayer. For instance, if you should decide, as an experiment, to give as much of yourself as you can to as much of God as you can grasp in this hypothesis, then the adventure is to try to live your whole life for a certain period *as if* you believed totally.

Some of the kinds of questions that come up immediately are: How do I relate to my family, friends, and business associates? How can I pray and find God's will as I begin to reorient my behavior after a serious commitment of my life and work to God?

This book consists of our observations made while trying to face some of the issues that actually came up in our lives as we began to take God seriously and personally. The chapters are made up of writings by each of us, often taken from books and articles we have written during the past twenty-six years. Interspersed with the material are questions we have raised with each other as we tried to relive our own adventures in preparing this book while living more than a thousand miles apart. If you would like to consider with us the questions we've faced in approaching a life focused on the God of Jesus Christ, imagine that you are thinking of beginning a whole new life. What would be involved as you stepped up to the edge of the adventure of faith and looked toward God?

BRUCE LARSON AND KEITH MILLER

Note: A related study aid for groups, *The Edge of Adventure: An Experiment of Faith,* is available through Villa Publishing Company, P.O. Box 26744, Austin, Texas 78755-0744. The thirteen-week study course—cassette and workbook—combined with this book is ideal for home or church group study.

REVISED EDITION

THE
EDGE
OF
ADVENTURE

CHAPTER ONE

❖

LIFE BEFORE A CHRISTIAN COMMITMENT

MEMORANDUM

TO: Bruce

FROM: Keith

RE: Chapter 1, Life Before a Christian Commitment

Do you remember, when I told you about the night during college I was walking down a deserted highway alone? I was choking back tears of frustration because I didn't know what to do with my life or why I was like I was. I wondered if anyone else had ever felt so screwed-up and lost?

I remember asking questions out loud to the sky: "Why do I do the things I do? Why do other people do what they do? *Who am I really*—behind the faces I show to the world? Does God care about me and the trap I'm in? And if he does, why doesn't he *change* me?" But then the disturbing thought came to me, "Do I really want to be changed *unless* I can call the shots as to how?"

Since these questions have come up again and again for both of us, I hope you'll include in the first section some of the material you've written concerning what life is meant to be. So many people have told me how fouled-up they feel as they face the kinds of questions we've had.

Why don't you start with what you think God's challenge is for the apparent hopelessness of man's situation in trying to determine what life is supposed to be?

K.

❖ I BELIEVE LIFE IS MEANT TO BE AN ADVEN-
ture. Thomas Carlyle said of someone, "He was born a man and
died a grocer." We humans, with so much potential for a loving,
joyful, meaningful existence, seem to have difficulty living up to
that potential. In my years in the parish, I have met so many men
and women of all ages and circumstances who are just muddling
through feeling defeated and overwhelmed by their problems.

One middle-aged man I know constantly carries a little black
book in his pocket where he records all of the unloving and
insensitive things that his wife has done to him over the years.

A high-powered executive in the advertising field told me that
he was retiring prematurely and hoped to spend the rest of his life
in a lighthouse. "For thirty years," he said, "I have been coping
with people and I have run out of cope."

A young woman who was devoted to God and who spent much
of her time working in the church and serving others contracted
an illness that kept her in bed for years. She describes her condition as, "I couldn't die and I couldn't get well."

A gifted clergyman confided one day, "The other night I woke
up and saw my wife sleeping beside me and I realized that there
was no way out of our hopeless relationship. Divorce is unthink-
able and I don't see how either of us can change. I love her, but
I don't know how to live with her."

At a funeral the widow confided that for several years her
husband had been sleeping with the lights on and a radio playing,
afraid to go to sleep lest he die. He weighed three hundred
pounds and had been told by his doctor that unless he dieted his
life was in danger. The more he feared death, the more he ate.
He died at fifty-five.

A young man getting a divorce after three years of marriage
seemed bewildered by his problems. "We thought we were meant
for each other. Before we were married she'd go sailing with me

and love it, and I used to enjoy going to hear her play in a string quartet. But now I get a headache whenever I hear chamber music and she gets seasick every time we go sailing."

A young suburban mother confessed to a small group that in spite of having five children, "I am not a good mother. I find that I don't enjoy children, not even my own."

A six-foot college student told several of us, "I love my parents very much and appreciate greatly all they have done for me, but I've never told them so. And I'm sure they love me, but they have never said so."

A young husband and father felt discouraged. "I am so ashamed of the way I treat my family. Why can't I be the man at home that I want to be?"

An executive reported on a conference he had attended focusing on creative relationships. "This team of social scientists asked us first of all to tell who we were, apart from our job or title. I found that I was unable to answer at all and that really scared me."

Who am I? Why do I do the things that I do? Why do other people do what they do? Is God concerned about me and the trap I am in? If he is, what can he do to help me? These are the most basic questions of life.

In the fifth chapter of the Book of John, we find a man trapped by life's circumstances. He had been ill for thirty-eight years and was looking for a cure. He spent his days beside a pool where the sick came from far and near. It was an authentic center of healing like Lourdes today or Saint Anne de Beaupré, or possibly was even the counterpart of one of our large medical clinics.

Jesus came to this place which was filled with human need. He walked among the patients and stopped beside this man who had been there for the greater part of his life and who had obviously been failed by the best medical and religious knowledge of his time. Jesus asks him an amazing question, "Do you *want* to be healed?" On the surface the question seems irrelevant and unfair. Of course this man wanted to be healed. He had spent most of his life in this place because healings occurred from time to time through curative waters.

However, instead of a simple yes or no, he said, in essence, "Sir, I perceive by your question that you have entirely missed the point. My problem is that the people I have been counting on to put me into the pool at the right time never seem to show up. They are always late." How much that man sounds like a great many of us when asked about our condition. We say, "You see, it's not my fault. My mother was a codependent. My father was seldom home. My employers have never appreciated me. My friends have let me down, and my wife doesn't understand me." There is something comfortable about the theory of "environmental conditioning" and even depth psychology that lets us off the hook. By blaming others for our present dilemmas, we miss the very key to escape.

As God encounters us in the midst of life's pressing situations, the issue is not our goodness or worthiness, for who is worthy before God and who is good enough?

As Jesus intrudes on this man's life, the real question is, Does he want to pay the price of being well? Though illness may be a great inconvenience, it has many fringe benefits. Illness can be a way to escape the drudgery of work and the burden of responsibility. Each day this man would watch his friends and contemporaries going off to work in hot fields and stifling shops, while he could lie in the cool of the porch beside the pool and discuss the news of the day with his friends or passersby.

When he was brought home each night, I'm sure he got preferential treatment from the family. We all know families in which we dare not upset Mother or Father who has high blood pressure or some other health problem. By being ill we can often get our way with people who would resist us if we competed on an equal basis.

Self-indulgence can be another fringe benefit. Things that we would not condone in others, we can excuse in ourselves if we are ill, in pain, or incapacitated. Illness is sometimes a way of getting attention, sympathy, or praise.

Some of these things may be involved in any illness. We can never assume that someone who is ill has an undivided desire to recover. Jesus simply asks this man if he dares to receive the gift of wholeness and begin to live and compete in the world on an equal basis. At some point in this dialogue (which is certainly not recorded in its entirety), the man by the pool must have answered yes. He is healed, picks up his bedroll, and walks into a new way of life.

In trying to understand the human predicament, we see, first, that at certain times all of us feel trapped by life in some seemingly hopeless situation that can stifle all joy and adventure and fulfillment. No one is immune. On the other hand, we believe in God's love for us, which is not conditioned by our goodness, and in his power to release and transform us. The basic question is, what are the things in us that prevent or block this healing and release?

An experience of mine during World War II has given me some helpful insights into our common predicament. I was a new infantry recruit at Fort Benning, Georgia. When I sat down to my first breakfast in the mess hall, with ten other men at a family-style table, I saw something in a large bowl that looked like cream of wheat. I scooped up a large amount in a bowl and poured on milk and sugar. A tall mountain boy sitting across from me was bug-eyed and said, "Is that the way you eat grits?"

As a Chicago boy I had heard of grits but had never seen them before. I filed this new information away for future reference. But rather than admit my ignorance, I smiled self-assuredly and said,

"Oh yes, this is how we eat grits in Chicago." He was amazed as I finished the bowl, which tasted terrible. But I kept my eye on him and discovered that the proper way to eat grits is with butter and salt.

Some days later I happened to be sitting at the same table with this same rangy mountaineer. Grits again were served that morning and under his watchful eye I took a bowl, scooped up some grits, and again poured on milk and sugar. Somehow I managed to eat the mess.

Part of the tragedy of the human predicament is demonstrated in this incident. We do not want to admit our mistakes. We would rather go to hell maintaining our innocence than to say, "I was wrong." Specific confession of sin seems to be extremely difficult for most of us in life's situations. Many in psychiatric work maintain that emotional and mental illness is often caused by our insistence that we are right. By admitting some error of long standing, we move toward maturity and healing. God asks us, "Do you want to be healed of some emotional or moral or physical ailment or do you want healing in some relationship?" When we can reply, "Yes, I have been wrong, I want to make things right and begin again," Jesus challenges us to take up our bed and walk. It may mean asking forgiveness or changing jobs or starting fresh in any number of costly ways.

Another factor in man's predicament is his desperate need for love. This perhaps underlies our defensiveness and refusal to admit error. Being made in the image of God, we are not like God, but made to need God and his love. We are meant for love and have an almost unlimited hunger for it. It is so important for us to be loved by family and friends and colleagues that we dare not reveal our imperfections lest we be rejected. We hide behind self-righteousness and pretense. It is this need for love that makes us destroy the very people for whom we care the most.

When I was a pastor in Illinois, I had a dog named Jock. He was a miserable dog who destroyed my wife's rugs and the neighbor's shrubs and the nocturnal peace of our whole street. But he had one outstanding quality—he loved me devotedly.

As I went to the church or the hospital or made calls, Jock used to follow my car and always arrived shortly after I did, much out of breath. I would pretend to be angry but inwardly I was pleased. I was sure there were few dogs that loved their masters as much as mine loved me.

All this time my wife kept saying a prophetic word, as wives have a way of doing. She pointed out that if Jock wasn't chained, or trained to stay at home, he would surely be run over someday. Someday came. He was killed and I was the one who killed him. He caught up to me at a stop sign and, not knowing he was there, I ran over him.

There is certainly truth in the old song, "You Always Hurt the One You Love." But it wasn't my love for Jock that destroyed him. It was my need for his love. As parents we destroy our children because we need them so much that we act not in their best interests but out of our needs. Jesus Christ offers to give us a new Spirit to motivate us and control us. This Spirit does not need people in this destructive way, but makes it possible for us to relate on the basis of the other's needs.

I cannot change the things in me that are most destructive. The question is, Am I willing to be changed? This "changing" is God's business. When we put ourselves into his hand, willing to be made new, we find that he is not only able but eager. Such is his love.

But what is the nature of the change that Christians sometimes call conversion? The parable of the prodigal son, perhaps the best-known parable, deals with such a change. We are told that "a certain man had two sons."

The story begins when the younger one asks his father for his share of the inheritance so that he can go out and make his fortune in the world. Most of us can identify with this young man in his search for the good life, for money, things, popularity, sex, status. He may simply have been looking for an escape from home and responsibilities. Most of us, apparently by nature, seek self-fulfillment through achievement in education, business, or society. We tend to prize material possessions and to see people as objects to be used in attaining those things. Perhaps the most damning evidence of man's unredeemed nature is that he manipulates people to acquire things.

Consistent with this, we find in the parable that the turning point in the young man's life is not a "religious experience." In returning to the father, the son is not motivated by repentance, grief, remorse, or insight. He merely becomes disgusted with his own material and social lot in life. He is hungry and cold and lonely, and he dares to believe that his father may still love him enough to provide him with the simple necessities. Jesus realized that conversion may not be in any sense a *religious* experience, but rather a *commonsense* experience. This is expressed flatly in the words, "He came to himself." The greatness of God's love is seen in his acceptance of people on these terms. Redemption for the prodigal also involved leaving the far country and starting the journey to his father's house. But the miracle of rebirth began at the point of common sense.

Jesus' story might also be called the parable of the two sons. Some of us see ourselves as the elder brother, the one who stayed home, worked hard, and was respectable in every way. But he was as lost as his younger brother, because he was working for wages and completely missing out on the marvelous gift of love and fellowship his father offered.

Too often marriage is seen as some sort of reciprocal arrangement. The husband or wife works for the approval of the other and misses the dynamic of real love. The marriage is based on the idea, "I will do this for you if you will do that for me."

The members of a family in one of my early parishes were considered the very "pillars of the church." Mother, father, and all the children were active, giving sacrificially of time, money, and leadership. One day the daughter was killed in an automobile accident while returning from a church conference. As far as I know, that family has not been inside the church since.

Motivation behind their religious devotion and church service seemed to be revealed. They had served God at great cost to themselves, hoping to put him in their debt and to buy some kind of insurance against the misfortunes of life. When God did not "keep his part of the bargain," they stopped serving him.

How many of us, like this family, or the elder brother in the parable, do the right things for the wrong reasons and miss the greatest gift that God has to give—the gift of his love!

Often the "elder brothers," "doing their duty," become the most unlovely people. In the parable, the elder brother complains to his father that he has never received a fatted calf with which to entertain his friends. One writer has suggested that he might have been able to entertain his friends with a single mutton chop.

Fulton Sheen once said, "God prefers a loving sinner to a loveless saint." This can be misunderstood, but we all know what he meant. In fact, I tend to find the prodigal son, even before his spiritual transformation, more lovable than his brother.

But the point of the parable is to teach us about the nature of God's love. Jesus described the unconditional love God has for us and challenges us to claim it. Commitment begins when we do that. It is the kind of love with which we are to love one another as we become a part of God's new creation.

MEMORANDUM

TO: Keith

FROM: Bruce

RE: Chapter 1, Life Before a Christian Commitment

As I looked over the material I'm just sending I realized that I may have raised more problems than I have spoken to in responding to your questions. For years you and I have discussed the problems of language and the fact that we so often have misunderstood the people around us (not to mention each other) because we have different meanings for the same word.

For instance, when I said that "commitment begins when we claim God's love," I could almost hear you saying, "Hmm, is *commitment* another word for 'conversion,' Bruce?"

So I'm hoping you'll respond with some of the ideas you've had when you thought about "claiming God's love." What is conversion? And what leads a person to the place in his search where he might turn to *God* for meaning and purpose in his life? Or more basically, is there *any* meaning and purpose "out there"? or even a God?

I guess the thing that is underneath all these more abstract questions about what God can do to *help* a person change is that deeper human question, When it's all over will things come out all right for people like me—and if so, how?

B.

❖ SEVERAL YEARS AGO I RESEARCHED ALL THE articles listed in the *Psychological Abstracts* on Christian conversion. I was interested in finding out what psychologists had discovered about the kinds of personality changes and hope men had experienced and attributed to having committed their lives to God.

I was surprised to discover that there are distinct traditions for both sudden and gradual Christian "conversions."

For some people conversion may seem to be sudden, like walking down the street, having the street break open, and falling through. For others the experience appears to be gradual. This gradual sort has been compared to the course of a sunflower as it turns imperceptibly toward the sun, but in the end is facing it.

But since all the accounts of Christian conversions which I read included the more dramatic life-changing type of experience, the following discussion will reflect that study. * And in the rest of this section I shall mean by the term *conversion* that identifiable experience through which a person becomes unified and consciously in right relationship with God, other people, and the world. The experience is accompanied by or closely associated with an act of personal "turning loose" or commitment to God, as he is revealed in Jesus Christ. This beginning results in a permanent reorientation toward God and toward trying to live the caring, vulnerable, and liberated life-style seen in Jesus.

I have come to believe that a *genuinely transforming conversion experience* is historically a relatively *rare thing* even among Christians. Therefore, the following picture may not relate to the experience of many people. But the effects of such deeply converted lives have been disproportionate with regard to their num-

---

* This is not dismissing gradual types of Christian change as valid. And as Bruce has pointed out, the "turning point" may be experienced as a common-sense decision. But to try to highlight the process often leading to conversion, I will be discussing here the more identifiable conversion experience.

ber in the church. So an attempt to reconstruct a modern inner map of the terrain and paths leading to conversion seems at least worth trying.

I shall draw a composite sketch from autobiographies, biographies, personal experiences, historical and other literary sources, and interviews with creative people who have reported Christian conversions in their own lives. This will be an "outline of a pilgrimage" toward being converted in the more dramatic or "sudden" way. There will of course be overlapping and reversals when compared to any specific life. And there may be omissions of certain "stages" in the life of any particular person heading toward conversion. But such oversimplification is apparently unavoidable in presenting models of an aspect of life which is dynamic and personal.

Man's condition, according to Christian tradition, is that he was created to be basically *good*, happy, and loving. We were made in the image of God (Genesis 1)—to be related to him. But in every case this image has been blurred. It seems that although we were originally designed to be free and loving, each of us chooses instead to spend his or her energies in various compulsive attempts to *be* God in our relationships to him, to other people, and to the material objects around us. We try to be the "most important one" and to control people around us in different ways. As the late Archbishop William Temple said, ". . . there is only one sin, and it is characteristic of the whole world. It is the self-will which prefers 'my' way to God's—which puts 'me' in the center where only God is in place."[1] As we do this, we become lonely pilgrims without knowing how it happened, somehow alienated from our given potential by a separation that extends to the core of our being. This *separation*, which Christianity says has been here since the first man, is called "sin."

The practical problem with trying to *be* God in one's own little world is that evidently no one can command the sort of universal approval and success the "role of God" calls for. It's an insatiable need. And regardless of the *size* of our achievements, we are left with a strange, lonely incompleteness or a sense that there has to be "more to life than this."

Paul Tillich[2] said that the state of our whole life is estrangement from others and ourselves—because we are estranged from the origin and aim of our lives. We do not know where we have come from or where we are going. So we try to create a controllable "game plan." We do this so we can repress our deep sense of separation. For if we think about it, we become terrified by such specters as the ultimate void of our own death and nothingness.

There are several basic problems like this which are so universal they appear to be built into the human mind. And even if we repress these questions, we seem to set out unconsciously to provide answers for ourselves. Or we try to structure our own little worlds in such a way that the queries never come up. Some of these questions are, Is reality evil and pushing toward death, or good and pressing toward hope? Does life have any meaning and purpose or is it a meaningless "tale told by an idiot"? What is the nature of the Really Real? And finally and most important, will everything come out all right in the end for me? Will life triumph over death somehow, or will death wear the grim (and only) smile at the end of the play?[3] The frantic rush of all our efforts seems to imply a fear that things will not come out all right in the end. So we hurry and build our kingdoms before we are defeated by death.

But I am getting ahead of my story. The point is that our "sensing," however vaguely, that life can be more than it is, sets up a tension inside us as we deal with the real world. This tension won't let us stop when our achievements have secured us enough to eat and drink. The intuitive feeling that we have a destiny beyond our present accomplishments provides the conscious motivating force which drives us toward ever greater goals.

Many people say that such a feeling of separation and tension is unhealthy. But as Viktor Frankl[4] has pointed out, some of this tension is an indispensable prerequisite of mental health. That is, it motivates people not to settle for physical comforts but to seek a more whole and complete condition. We are, it seems, on an unconscious search for liberation and wholeness.

A strange feature of this struggle is that each of us evidently feels that his own basic tenseness and anxiety about the incompleteness of life is somehow unique. However, as psychologist George Kisker said, this condition of anxious unsettledness is true for almost everybody most of the time.

But the average person will probably *not* see the source of his deep lack of satisfaction as resulting from a separation from God. We more often interpret our restlessness as due to our *lack of achievement* or our inability to get control of our environment. We cannot manipulate the people around us completely enough to have them fulfill our needs for physiological goodies, security, affirmation, and esteem—which will, we feel, be met through achievements, conquests, and acquisitions of various kinds. When we are young, our "progress" may be fast enough that we can avoid or repress conscious anxiety—believing we will continue to succeed through what appears to be an endless sea of time ahead of us.

During all this striving and achieving we may have no consciousness of God. But the Christian belief is that our basic problem is *not* lack of achievement in our external environment and that we are doomed to frustration. Besides, Christians believe that our strong bent toward glorifying ourselves will make us foul our own inner nest—even when we have succeeded magnificently in manipulating our environment.

Paul Tournier[5] describes this inner bent by saying that man left to himself is lost. Our own efforts, our own goodwill and good intentions, our own virtues cannot banish our "disease." We are aware that even our most sincere efforts to banish disease bring new evils in their train. There seems to be a poison within us, given with life itself and present throughout its duration, which contaminates almost every experience in advance.

At some point in this confusing pattern of achieving and fouling our own nests, a person's "search" may take on a new quality of intensity. This happens when the image of life and success we have invested with ultimate importance is threatened with destruction. This may take place either because we are failing in a way we can't avoid admitting *or* because we have *reached* our goals and succeeded. If we had counted on "achievement" to solve our basic self-alienation and meet our dominant needs, we may be depressed when success is unmistakable, but does *not* bring the relatedness and wholeness we dreamed of. If, on the other hand, our failure is stark and apparently irreversible, the psychological effect may be very similar. In either case we have misread our world. Somehow we bet all our happiness and fulfillment capital on the wrong horse.

But part of our bent toward playing God makes it amazingly difficult to admit even to ourselves that we have been wrong in our important judgments. Many of us also find it hard to ask help from another person with regard to our own personal problems. So when the time comes that we must *face* our failure or success, several things may happen to us: Because our own efforts or preconceived solutions to the riddle of life have failed to bring happiness, we may for the first time become conscious of the self-defeating nature of our success-oriented life-style. And we may become poignantly aware of our need for "outside help." But there is often a desperate internal struggle before this realization becomes conscious. Most of us repress this need for help, even when it is very obvious to the people around us. I have seen again and again how much tragedy and pain I could have avoided if I had gone to someone for help sooner.

Thomas Gordon[6] has described this battle against the conscious discovery of the mistaken foundation stones on which one has tried to build his life. He says that there seems to be something in human nature—whether learned and acquired or rooted in the organic makeup of all living organisms—something that predisposes us to defend our world of reality against the threat of change. We seek the type of experience that supports our present stance and reject experiences—even potentially helpful ones—that seem to promise a disturbance of the current direction for our lives.

Because of this great resistance to change, it is usually only when our old personal world is threatened with destruction or meaninglessness that we may be open to taking seriously a radical change in our life's *purpose* and *direction*. Only when we are somehow blocked in this way will we ordinarily consider a "higher" personal power which might make whole that which is separated in us and find that which is lost.

What apparently happens when our old world is seriously threatened is that a person's search changes from a conscious wish for *specific solutions*—means and material assistance toward the fulfillment of achievement goals—to search for overall *healing* and *hope* for *himself* or *herself*. Thoughts change from, "How can I get this project finished," to, "I'm confused and miserable and need some help from somewhere to get through today." And Christian tradition indicates that we must have this realization of the need for profound change and for help to accomplish it. These are two of the primary conditions that make a person ready for a new vision of life and of God.

But William James[7] said that besides the feeling of present incompleteness or wrongness from which one is now eager to escape, there must be a growing awareness that there may be something "out there" to respond to—which we have been too busy to notice before. And I found in almost every "case history" there was this dawning awareness of something beyond their own minds—whether the person involved had previously experienced close contact with Christianity or not.

The common feeling of being almost irresistibly drawn toward a presence or force beyond themselves seems to be the common experience of all kinds of people as they face the awareness of their own limited humanity. John Knox[8] talks about what common meaning the term *God* may have for different kinds of people as they become aware of the possibility of something to which they might relate beyond themselves. "What, for example," he asks, "is the 'obsession' which Gamaliel Bradford describes as a 'keen, enormous, haunting, never-sated thirst for God'? When Francis Thompson tells of his flight from the 'hound of heaven,' *what* is pursuing him? When Bertrand Russell cries out that in the 'center of (him) is always and eternally a terrible pain,' a 'searching for something beyond what the world contains,' what is this something? When Augustine said, 'Thou has made us for thyself and we are restless till we rest in thee,' of whom, or to whom, was he speaking? It is obvious from these examples—that the word *God* may have the most poignant meaning even for one who doubts or denies his objective reality as an actual being or existence. Bertrand Russell—having spoken of 'something transfigured and infinite, the beatific vision, God,' goes on to say, 'I do not find it, I do not think it is to be found, but the love of it is my life.' "

But even as the potential convert feels a yearning or drawing toward something beyond his own life, he begins to sense a strong resistance within himself to responding to this unknown being or power. This again seems to be a part of our desperate need to be king or god of our own personal worlds. We want to be *helped* and *loved* by God, but we fear that he will absorb us or we will lose our identity and "control" if we get too close to him. We are afraid that he will make us "religious," "unnatural," vulnerable to the ridicule of those whose approval we've always sought. Or as Sören Kierkegaard said, we are afraid that we might live to regret responding to God.

But having tried on our own and realized our human limitations, having faced the inadequacy of our past view of life, and having sensed a calling or yearning toward "a person" or presence beyond ourselves, we may be almost ready for Christian conversion.

But before this can happen, it seems that there must be an internal "showdown" leading to a personal crisis of the will. This crisis involves the necessity for us to take a gigantic psychological leap: to acknowledge frankly our sense of worthlessness. Psychologist Hobart Mowrer[9] in a non-Christian context talks about the necessity and difficulty of honest confession before a new wholeness is possible for a patient in therapy: ". . . we encounter difficulty because human beings do not change radically until they first acknowledge their sins, but it is hard for one to make such an acknowledgment unless he has 'already changed.' In other words, the full realization of deep worthlessness is a severe 'ego insult,' and one must have a new source of strength to endure it." So before we can confess at this depth we usually must have determined at a level unconscious to ourselves that God is real—that he is really "out there."

This difficulty in honestly facing and confessing our helplessness can lead us into an internal struggle that may last for a few hours or for years—until we can envision a new source of strength available to us. Generally the motivation to go on and confess is provided in one of two ways (and often this is where the Christian witness comes in): the struggler may meet a person whose converted life or words about God's loving acceptance and power attract him. This Christian's faith and confidence may reinforce the struggler's yearning *enough* that he can overcome the fear of surrendering himself (and the god position in his life) to God.

If he does not meet such a Christian, there is another route to the crisis point: the anxiety of the struggle may be *heightened* by either circumstances or communication. We may hear in a sermon or begin to suspect that we are *never* going to make it by ourselves. A kind of terror can surface. At that point a frightening confrontation may be precipitated. A genuine religious conversion is evidently the outcome of a crisis. Though this encounter may take place in different circumstances and forms and there may be many preparatory steps, the event of conversion comes to focus in a crisis of ultimate concern. There is in such a conversion a sense of desperate conflict in which one is so involved that his whole meaning and destiny are at stake in a "life or death," all-or-none significance. Unless a person is aware of a conflict serious enough to defeat him, and unless he is concerned ultimately enough to put his life in the balance, he is not ready for conversion.*

So assume that we reach a crisis, confess our self-centeredness and our sense of worthlessness, and really want a new life. Almost all Christian traditions maintain that the next step after confession is *repentance*. But Christian repentance is *not* a mere verbal expression or being "sorry about" certain acts. It is more like an agonizing wrenching as we turn our backs on our own past. It's as if we were pulling our lives up by the roots and replanting them,

---

* See William James, *The Varieties of Religious Experience* (New York: Random House, 1902), p. 186 f. Other kinds of crucial change, failure, or tragedy (*e.g.*, divorce, death of a loved one) can precipitate a conversion crisis. But unless the crisis includes the integral elements in the process described here, the resulting conversion may be only a part of the grief reaction. And such "conversions" often evaporate when the crisis is over.

facing in a different direction. This act of will constitutes a deep denial of our past direction and becomes a first step toward responding to the God we have sensed was pursuing us.

To summarize the pilgrimage so far: the description of a pre-conversion person pictured a striving man or woman, confident at first that without help he or she could find or create the conditions for self-fulfillment. But our attempts to manipulate people and our environment toward material or social success and acclaim finally teach us that we are only human and that our humanity yearns for a kind of relatedness and completion beyond ourselves and our manipulations. We may first experience frustration, then anxiety. And our inner crying out for help, new direction, and meaning may change the focus of our lives from a preoccupation with means to our success-oriented goals to a global need for being saved from the swamp in which our motivational feet are stuck. As this condition approaches consciousness, we may become ready to *confess* our helpless sense of separation and realize that we need to *repent* (or turn from) our past life-style and direction. This sequence may be unconscious until the moment of conversion, or one may be aware of the overall progression described here.

If a person can identify with several parts of the process described so far, he may be a candidate for a profound Christian conversion.

CHAPTER TWO

❖

TAKING THE GAMBLE —COMMITMENT

MEMORANDUM

TO: Bruce

FROM: Keith

RE: Chapter 2, Taking the Gamble—Commitment

Now that I've said I think there are some basic things that might happen to people which could cause them to consider changing their old or inadequate game plan or life direction, why don't you put in some of the ideas you've written about the difference between a serious belief as an "intellectual exercise" and as a "call to experiment." The older I get, the more I am convinced that the *big* life decisions are the risking kind you described to me on the phone.

How does a normal, "nontheological" type man or woman answer the call to experiment? And if one begins, what direction does the commitment take, what does the beginning involve, and what will it "cost"? (You know, it's occurring to me in trying to bring up questions like that in this unlikely book why more people haven't.) What is an experiment as opposed to a "head belief"?

K.

❖ A STORY I HEARD A LONG TIME AGO DEM-
onstrates for me some of the essential ingredients of any serious
commitment and also illustrates some of the differences in belief
as an intellectual exercise and a living experiment.

The following letter was found in a baking powder can wired
to the handle of an old pump that offered the only hope of
drinking water on a very long and seldom-used trail across the
Amargosa Desert:

"This pump is all right as of June 1932. I put a new sucker
washer into it and it ought to last five years. But the washer dries
out and the pump has got to be primed. Under the white rock I
buried a bottle of water, out of the sun and cork end up. There's
enough water in it to prime the pump, but not if you drink some
first. Pour about one fourth and let her soak to wet the leather.
Then pour in the rest medium fast and pump like crazy. You'll
git water. The well has never run dry. Have faith. When you git
watered up, fill the bottle and put it back like you found it for the
next feller. (signed) Desert Pete

"P.S. Don't go drinking up the water first. Prime the pump
with it and you'll git all you can hold."

Nowhere have I seen the principles of faith more clearly set
forth. What a person would do coming along that trail, half dead
from lack of water and with an empty canteen, would reveal
much about his faith. Faith is not so much an academic subject
for discussion or a theological term from the Bible, as it is something on which our very life hinges.

As reflected in this story, faith is evidently composed of three
ingredients. First, there must be an object. It is impossible just "to
have faith." If you were a lonely traveler coming down that
parched desert trail, you would have to trust in an unknown person
named Desert Pete to keep from drinking the buried bottle of
water. This would not be easy. He is a person you do not know.

There is a great deal of evidence he is telling the truth, but there is no guarantee that he is not a practical joker or a lunatic. So, the first ingredient of faith is trust in someone or something, based on evidence but not infallible proof.

The second ingredient is risk. Faith is always costly. If you were walking down the trail without water, there would be nothing more precious to you in all the world than a bottle of water. Desert Pete tells you that if you drink any part of that bottle of water he has left, you won't get any from the pump. So, it seems necessary to risk the very stuff on which your life may depend to get a safe and sufficient amount. Faith is always expensive.

The third ingredient is work. Some people have mistakenly interpreted faith as a substitute for work. Faith is not laziness. Desert Pete reminds us that after we trust and risk, we have to pump hard!

Everyone uses faith daily. We must trust our partners in marriage or in business although sometimes that trust is misplaced. In business, money and reputation are risked; in marriage, your whole life. For success, both a business and a marriage require a tremendous amount of work and consecration by both parties.

So much for faith. But what about Christian faith? The ingredients are the same. First of all, one has to have faith in God and especially in the way God has revealed himself to man in the person of Jesus Christ. It is not faith in a principle but faith in a person—the Person!

Second, there is commitment that involves risk. Anything approaching a total commitment always has specific and immediate implications that involve risk. It may mean asking forgiveness of another, making a specific restitution, beginning to tithe, or changing jobs. The more we commit of ourselves to God in very specific terms, the better we can know him and his plan for our lives.

Third, there is hard work. After one has had faith in God and tried to commit his or her life to him, then comes the hard work. Some people have interpreted the Christian faith as just a matter of hard work. This leads to a kind of living which may be religious, but is not necessarily Christian. Christian faith is more than hard work for Christ and his Kingdom. But I have never known an effective Christian who was lazy.

In the Bible, Abraham has been called the Father of the Faithful. Because of his faith in God he left his home in Ur of the Chaldees. By faith he gave up the known and the familiar for the unknown and unfamiliar. He committed his life and his family and all of his possessions to the leadership of God, who called him to a new life in a new land. To find that new land and the new life required years of hard work. Many of the men and women of faith in the Bible have had similar experiences.

In the New Testament, we read about the call to commitment which Jesus extended to the first disciples and we find, first of all, that it was (and, I think, still is) a person-to-person call. They were not called to believe a doctrine, practice an ethic, or worship in a prescribed way. Rather, they were called to trust Jesus and follow him.

The original call was not to people who could be considered "spiritual types," those who naturally enjoy prayer, meditation, and the esthetics of worship. Instead, Jesus called men who were virile, earthy, and ordinary. We might have expected him to call people with "time on their hands"—the rich, the unemployed, or the retired—but instead he called middle-class businessmen with vested interests. Certainly our Lord calls people with a spiritual bent, but he is no respecter of persons. Men and women from every walk of life who are willing to respond are called.

How odd, too, that no time limit was implied in that original call. Jesus merely asked four fishermen to follow him. Did they interpret this as an invitation for that day, or for a week, or possibly for several years? When they left their businesses, their friends, their familiar surroundings, and even their families to follow Jesus Christ, they could not have known it was to be a lifetime call.

A certain layman has been one of the pioneers in land reapportionment in the world's underdeveloped areas, working for the United Nations and for private foundations. His leadership improved conditions for thousands, and he has personally introduced scores of people to a Living Christ.

He tells an almost incredible story of his original call. Intrigued by a group of Christians and dissatisfied with much of his own life, he was at first frightened by the totality of Christian commitment. One of his new friends asked if he would consider turning his life over to Christ's management for a one-week trial.

"That's too long," was his reply.

"How about one day?"

"Can't do it."

"How about one hour?"

Hesitatingly, he said yes. You can guess the rest. Since that moment he hasn't lived life on the old terms.

In the New Testament the message seems clear that the new life offered by Jesus Christ begins when we repent and believe.

Repentance is the time of "coming to one's self" as the prodigal son did. It is the moment of truth when we realize that our goals and our methods are false and that we are not truly happy or fulfilled. C. S. Lewis said, "The hunger that the Lord has given you is the best gift you have." As we sit in the far country, we realize that we have been looking in the wrong place for what is lasting and true and worthwhile. Repentance for the prodigal, however, did not mean merely a sense of regret, but enough disgust with his own condition to make him get up and start the journey home.

Belief for the Christian is not intellectual exercise, but rather a call to experiment. We test God's love to see whether he is a faithful father who will provide for all of our needs and take us back into his household again. Our whipping takes place in the far country, not in the household of God. We have been punished, and when we return to God, he lavishes upon us all those things we do not deserve but need so desperately. The root of sin is our refusal to be loved by God or to be part of his household, or to have fellowship with him. Belief, or faith, means turning to God as he is revealed in Jesus Christ, and testing his nature.

A housewife was challenged by some friends in a small group to turn her life over to God. In all honesty she replied that this was impossible because her life was crammed with activities and obligations. Finally she agreed to an experiment. She would mark off one day on her calendar and she would give that day to God. When the fateful day came, she found she was unable to get out of bed because she felt ill. The doctor diagnosed her trouble as some very minor thing, but advised her to rest. Spending the day in bed, she realized that the thing she feared God would ask of her was even more "busyness." Instead, he had given her a day of rest to renew her body, mind, and spirit.

Finally, commitment in simple terms seems to mean entering into a right relationship with God. Belief is more than merely accepting Christian doctrine. One can be doctrinally sound and relationally handicapped, crippled, or impotent. It is quite possible to know all the classic Christian teachings about the nature of God and his dealings with mankind and still treat him as though he were irrelevant to or far removed from real life.

A right relationship means that one has heard the Good News that God says to us in Jesus Christ: "I love you. I love you as you are. I love you unconditionally. I have already given myself to you totally, and now all I ask is that you begin to respond to my love and my commitment to you by committing to me all of yourself that you are able to give."

God's love does not depend on any virtue in us or on our achievements. But, as I understand it, the nature of his love is such that he does not leave us as he finds us. When someone begins the adventure of faith, God says to him, in effect: "I am going to begin to change you. Programmed into your inner computer, through glands and genes and circumstances and experiences, is an inability to love totally. I love you so much that I want to change all of those intricate wires of experience, sense, and thought that make you an unknowable, unrelatable person. It may take a thousand years of reprogramming to make you a lover of people, of me, and of yourself, but I promise that I will continue relentlessly until you have been totally transformed. I'll begin at the moment you give me your life, and I will not stop until all your quirks and defense mechanisms and subterfuges and alibis are gone and you are a transparent, relatable person."

This is what I hear God saying in the gospel.

And more: "But even after a thousand years of this process of change, I will not love you one bit more than I love you now, at the moment of your commitment to me; or one bit more than I loved you at the moment of your conception or your birth. My love for you is total and unconditional. I am not trying to change you so that I can love you. I love you, and because I do, I want you to experience this change."

If this is what the Cross is all about, if this is what Jesus Christ has accomplished by his Incarnation and Atonement, then we are talking about Good News that is almost too good to be true.

MEMORANDUM

TO: Keith

FROM: Bruce

RE: Chapter 2, Taking the Gamble—Commitment

When I was putting the material together about answering the call to experiment, I made a note to remind you to describe your own personal "trip" at this point. It seems to me that my problems with really considering a seriously committed life have stemmed from the fact that I couldn't find anyone who seemed "like me" who took God all that seriously.

What happens to a contemporary person who says yes in the far country? What does it feel like inside and where does he go? (Specifically what happened to you and where did you go?)

B.

❖ How does one describe a new beginning with God as the motivating center of his life without basing his description on some vague mystical feeling? How does a person who wants to have intellectual integrity describe the experience of encountering God existentially as the personal, the immediate, and limitless *Thou* in his or her life? The attempt to explain this unfolding in a layman's contemporary experience is complicated by the fact that Christ did not leave a reasoned theological explanation. All he seems to have pointed to and promised his followers was a *"way"*—a way across the chasm between God and them, between them and others . . . and between people and their real nature.

The gospel of Jesus Christ calls for a different understanding of the nature of truth than most of us have been educated to have. Where the scientific method has been dominant in a Christian layman's education, he sometimes thinks of God as a Master-Thinker, or Philosophical Theologian. In a real sense I believe God is presented in the Christian revelation as more of a living and creative artist than a philosopher or theologian. A philosopher in order to be universal presents an argument or dialogue covering every possible contingency; but an artist in attempting to be universal is terribly specific. For example, to describe the universal experience of frustration, or of questioning about life, a poet gives us a picture of one specific mouse in a field, one Grecian urn, one country churchyard . . . and in these specific scenes or experiences all men can see frustration, and the basic mystery of their own lives.

Christianity says that when God wanted to convey the truth about his infinite love for all people he made that love incarnate in a *single* life . . . and in the action of that life all kinds of people have been able to perceive his love's universal extent through the enlightening work of God's Spirit. History has shown again and again that in trying to transmit the essence of the *Life* Christ demonstrated and continues to offer each of us, we cannot speak adequately in propositional terms. We are forced to turn to the language of living experience. In the last analysis we are all reduced to the witness of "that which we have seen and heard" in our own lives.

I do not know any "general rules" for living life as a businessman and father and husband consciously committed to the Living Christ. I know of no scholars in this field. All I can do is to witness to insights received on one adventure of faith that continues to change my own life and that of my family. The fact that these insights have been verified in the Scriptures, in the lives of Christians in the church's history, and in the experience of dozens of contemporary men and women I know has made me believe that they represent more than a subjective pilgrimage. This is the way it began:

By the time I was eighteen years old I was a great success. (At least at the time it seemed that I was.) In a large high school I had won honors in basketball, dramatic reading, class plays, had been elected president of the senior class, and finally king of the school. Life's opportunities appeared to be limitless, in spite of the fact that it was 1945 and we were in the midst of the Second World War.

Three months after graduation, I saw the Western world sitting on the brink of an explosion of joy and relief, anticipating momentarily the official word that the war was over. But fifteen days before the war ended we received word that my only brother, whom I idolized, had been killed in a plane crash while serving in the air force. That night I remember sitting alone on the back steps in tears.

We had always been a close family, and my mother's reaction was one of deep grief, as was my father's. As I sat there terribly alone, I felt that someday I had to find the meaning of life. I felt that I had to pour myself into it twice as much, since Earle would not get a chance to live it at all. During those next few months my mother got continually worse, and finally had a nervous breakdown a little over a year later. The strain on my father had been too much also, and at about the same time he had a heart attack. I had left for the navy two weeks after my brother's death, and after eleven months I had been released to go to college. My parents were sick; and as I began to get to know them as one adult knows others, they poured out their souls separately before me. I realized that although I had been living with them nineteen years, I did not really know these people—nor did they know each other. They did not realize the anguish caused by the little things in their own lives which hurt and frustrated each other; and I felt that neither actually understood about the hopes and dreams in the other's soul . . . and yet we had been a close family and had known much love and happiness. I began to realize that there was a great deal of life that I had not counted on.

I went to college on a basketball scholarship and the G.I. bill. During the Christmas vacation of my sophomore year I was traveling across the state to a fraternity party. We were driving very fast when the right front wheel slipped off onto the highway shoulder that had been washed away. The driver tried to turn the car suddenly back onto the highway, and it went completely out of control. There was a long screech, and I closed my eyes.

Suddenly, I felt like a rock in a tin can as we bounced and rolled 270 yards down a long hillside, over and over, five and a half times. When the car stopped it was on its side and I was on my face against the groundward side. There was dust everywhere. I lay still for a moment and then opened my eyes. There, beside me, was a pair of legs, and I thought my friend who had been riding with me in the backseat had been cut in two. But then the legs began to move and I realized he had been thrown facefirst out the rearview window and was struggling to pull his legs free.

When he got out and turned around, he smiled. His skin seemed to sort of fall apart from the impact. Blood was covering his face.

I tried to get up on my hands and knees but my head fell, and I realized that I had broken my neck. I kept trying to think, "What happens to you when you break your neck?" All I could remember was that you died. Somehow I wanted to get out of that car to die.

It was just about sunset, and the cold grayness of December was closing in around us. I told my friend what had happened, and then asked him if he could help me get out. He was unhurt except for facial cuts. So I held my head with both hands, realizing that I had to keep my spine straight, and he dragged me out of the car. I remember as he was trying to help me, looking around and seeing spectators standing around the car watching, afraid to help for fear of becoming involved. One man was even taking a photograph, and I thought to myself, "What a cold bunch of —— these are!"

My friend, Bob, put his overcoat on the ground and helped me lie down beside the road, then covered me with my own coat. I lay there an hour and a half waiting for the ambulance. I remember lying beside the highway and praying very simply. I was very much awake. As I prayed I had a strange feeling of peace that permeated my consciousness. I thought to myself, "What a shame to find out that this kind of peace is a reality so late in life." For the first time I was not afraid to die. I realized at that moment that even in this tragedy which might be the end of life for me there was Something very personal, very real which was more important than anything else I had ever known.

But I got over the broken neck . . . and the feeling of peace.

The next couple of years were filled with turmoil inside, and yet a turmoil mingled with a great deal of joy. For although I was bearing the burdens of the family in trying to keep my parents afloat emotionally and spiritually as their lives were drawing to an end, I also found and fell in love with a girl at school, whose love changed my life. Although I had recovered from my broken neck, I had also pushed God back into the corner of my life as I reentered the stream of competition for grades and attention. Except that by now a lot of that frantic life had lost its savor. Some of the fresh naïveté had been replaced by methodical knowledge of how to get things done in the world of people. In my sophomore year I was elected president of my fraternity, and found out that I was on the verge of having ulcers the same month.

Not many months later I remember sitting in a hospital room, beside the bed of my father who was dying. I was praying again and wringing my hands in helpless frustration. His stomach ulcers had perforated, and because of his heart condition they could not operate. I was sitting beside his bed watching him bleed to death internally. I loved him very much. As I sat there helplessly shaking my head, a small Roman Catholic nun, one of the Sisters at the hospital, came into the room. She walked over to the other side of my father's bed, picked up his hand, and patted it. She said to him gently, "Can you hear me?"

He said, "Yes," very weakly.

She said to him, "Have you ever accepted Jesus Christ as your Lord and Savior?"

He shook his head, "No."

Then she asked him quietly and matter-of-factly, "Would you like to do this?"

There was a pause and then he said, "Oh *yes*."

She said to him, "Then repeat after me: I accept you, Jesus Christ, as my Lord and Savior."

He did, and then he twisted in the bed and died.

After my father's death I graduated from college and went to work for a major oil company. I had married Mary Allen in my senior year. We were sent to that company's exploration office in southwest Texas, near the Rio Grande valley. In those next months as I drove through that vast desert land near the Mexican border, I came to love the silence, the stillness, and the vastness very much. I became fascinated by the changes in the desert. The white-hot-noonday blast with the heat waves rising continually and visibly off the highway ahead and off the desert to the side would change into an amazing coolness. The magnificent sunsets hinted at something wonderful and very real beyond the horizon. Then suddenly the total blackness of night and coldness would envelop it all. As I drove through that vast desert country alone, day after day, I began to sense something of the majesty and the silent power of God in the world. There awoke in me a realization that I must somehow learn more about God and find out about Jesus Christ—who was supposed to *be* God.

This restlessness grew until one night at home in the middle of the night I woke Mary Allen and said, "Honey, I've got to go back to school to find out about God."

She was sleepy and surprised, but after a moment said, "I'll go with you, but how will we do it?"

We had a new baby and some debts to pay. I said I didn't know but thought maybe we ought to pray about it, and we did. I did not have any desire to become an ordained minister but that seemed to be what the kind of interest I had had, pointed to. This seemingly was what one did when his commitment and interest reached a certain point.

When the men at the oil company office found out that I was going to study theology, many of them did not know quite how to react. I was the first person from that office to go to divinity school. They didn't know how to send me off. They had a way which was standard for sending people off to other offices. They didn't know if this would be appropriate. But since there was no precedent for a change, the final social functions engineered by our friends were empowered by the usual spirits, which did not seem at all incongruous at the time.

I remember one of my closest friends at the office putting his arm around my neck and leaning rather heavily on me at about two o'clock one morning and saying to me through deeply sincere and slightly watery eyes, "Buddy, you'll never make it!" And with this send-off we went to live in the East.

I had enrolled in a graduate theological school, realizing that God, that Reality, must lie in this direction. The church said that it did and the world thought that it might. Off we went.

But regardless of any preparation we had had, when we got to the school I soon sensed that for me there was something terribly wrong at divinity school. Some of these young men seemed more full of themselves than had the men at the fraternity to which I belonged. There seemed to be an intellectual competitiveness that was very keen, and somehow unloving. But this I understood, and began to try to compete with the best of them. As the weeks rolled by I felt in my soul that this couldn't be the answer to life, since it was only a religious version of the same kind of competitiveness I already *knew* did not end in Reality. Some of the seminarians began to talk about being ordained, and their interests were in some cases focused on things I considered to be quite trivial . . . how long must one's surplice be . . . whose wife could make the most beautiful stoles for the various seasons of the year—none about which I could care less!

When I had arrived at school I didn't know the *answers* to the theological questions we were trying to discuss, but I did know the *questions* people ask when they're dying and when they are afraid. And if God through the church didn't have the answers to these questions, then how could he be God? I wanted to know how we could get to know God *personally* in such a way that we could have something of the Holy Spirit in our lives.

I felt that a man who was a minister should know God so well that when he came into someone's living room he could sit down quietly and open his soul in such a way that God's love in his life would create a real hunger for Reality in the souls of the other people there and lead them to God too. I sensed intuitively that there must be a way to introduce God into other people's lives . . . that this must somehow be what it's all about. But everywhere I found that people wanted to intellectualize the Good News, wanted to make it conceptual or make it propositional and in any case to stay away from personal confrontation. And somehow in those intellectualized arguments, the aliveness of God would evaporate and fade away, only to come back into my soul when I was alone in prayer.

I studied hard and was as interested as any of them in the academic work; but I was repelled by the lack of gut-level engagement with the problems of the rawness of living out one's days and nights as a businessman and husband and citizen. I felt we were dealing with the awesome God of Moses and the Intellectual Power of the Greeks; but nowhere did I see the personal redeeming God of Jesus Christ.

After four terms of this I realized that whatever it was that was the matter (I did not know), I could not in good conscience be ordained. Mary Allen had had a second baby that fall after my third term. She almost died following the birth of this baby. She was desperate and lonely, 1,700 miles from home; and I was very little help. I was in a state of turmoil inside that no one knew about, and I began to fear for my sanity. I was trying to take care of our two babies and go to classes. Mary Allen was in the hospital, very sick and frightened. Inside, my soul was like a tableau of warriors by Michelangelo, the figures twisting and turning for release. Finally I realized I had to get out of there. I completed the term; and we left.

The oil company had said we could come back if I ever wanted to work for them again, and I called. They were very kind, but suddenly I realized something for the first time: when a young man in our generation went off to the seminary, although most of his contemporaries didn't really understand, they thought it was fine for him. But when he came back, having left the seminary, they didn't understand.

Because of my tremendous self-centeredness and pride, I have always tried desperately to be understood. The oil company took me back and sent us to the office we had been in before. I would rather have gone to almost any other place, because this "going back" represented my first great human failure. There was no way I could explain to the people around me what had gone on and was going on inside my soul, behind the confident mask I showed to the world. I began to work, because I had a wife whom I loved very much and two babies I loved deeply. But there seemed to be no hope, no ultimate purpose, anymore. If there was a God, the people at the seminary had subtly hinted that I must have turned away from him (or perhaps this was my imagination). At any rate I felt things closing in on me in the inner chamber of my life.

I used to walk down the streets, I remember, and suddenly would break out in a cold sweat. I thought I might be losing my mind. One day it was so bad that I got in my company car and took off on a field trip alone. As I was driving through the tall pine woods country of East Texas I suddenly pulled up beside the road and stopped. I remember sitting there in complete despair. I had always been an optimistic person, and had always had the feeling that there was "one more bounce in the ball." After a good night's sleep, or perhaps a couple of martinis and a good night's sleep, one could always start again tomorrow. But now there was no tomorrow in my situation. I was like a man on a great gray treadmill going no place, in a world that was made of black, black clouds all around me.

As I sat there I began to weep like a little boy, which I suddenly realized I was inside. I looked up toward the sky. There was nothing I wanted to do with my life. And I said, "God, if there's anything you want in this stinking soul, take it."

This was years ago. But something came into my life that day which has never left. There wasn't any ringing of bells or flashing of lights or visions; but it was a deep intuitive realization of what it is God wants from a person, which I had never known before. And the peace that came with this understanding was not an experience in itself, but was rather a cessation of the conflict of a lifetime. I realized then that God does not want a person's money, nor does he primarily want time, even the whole lifetime of it a young seminarian is ready to give him. God, I realized, doesn't want your time. He wants your *will*; and if you try to give him your will, he'll begin to show you life as you've never seen it before.

For me it was like being born again. I saw that I had not seen Christ at seminary because I had never known God personally.

As I sat there I continued to cry, only now the tears were a release from a lifetime of being bound by myself, by the terrific drive to prove that I am something—*what* I had never quite understood. Although I could not understand or articulate for many months what had happened to me, I knew to the core of my soul that I had somehow made personal contact with the very Meaning of Life.

I started the car and turned toward home.

MEMORANDUM

TO: Bruce

FROM: Keith

RE: Chapter 2, Taking the Gamble—Commitment

After looking over the story of my own beginning which you asked for, I realized that my research on conversion indicates that there are *many* different ways a one might answer the call to commitment when it comes to one's own consciousness.

Some people have been converted in large meetings or small groups, others in cathedral confirmation classes. But in every case, I am convinced that everyone must respond individually—even if there are a thousand people around at the time. So I've included the following additional descriptive material on the actual experience of conversion.

I have met a number of people who didn't really believe I was a Christian because my description of what I did and said in my response to God's call was not like theirs. I hope the enclosed will at least take us out of that trap.

K.

❖ ALTHOUGH IT HAS BEEN DESCRIBED IN many ways, this "reply to God" evidently is an attempt at a *specific* and *total commitment* of our future to him.

Many Christian teachers have urged moderation in speaking of the necessity of such a specific commitment, realizing that this more radical conversion is not likely to be the experience of everyone. But Dietrich Bonhoeffer was quite clear in stating the necessity for a definite act at this point. "Unless a definite step is demanded, the call vanishes into thin air; and if men imagine that they can follow Jesus without taking this step they are deluding themselves. . . ."[1]

And this act is not merely saying yes to a proposition or creed about God. But as Martin Marty noted, it means "being grasped." Inside, it is the feeling of *responding*, not of instigating. One feels that *God* is offering the relationship. And this offering on God's part before we have offered, so to speak, is called God's "grace."[2]

Man's specific response has been called in poetic language: "Opening the door (of one's personal life) to Christ." John Stott spells out the difference between this specific opening of one's self and other religious activities when he says that "this step is the beginning and nothing else will do instead. You can believe in Christ intellectually and admire Him; you can say your prayers to Him through the keyhole (as I did for many years)*; you can push coins at Him under the door; you can be moral, decent, upright and good; you can be religious and pious; you can have been baptized and confirmed; you can be deeply versed in the philosophy of religion; you can be a theological student and even an ordained minister—and still not have opened the door to Christ. There is no substitute for this."[3]

But here again is the baffling paradox of people seeking—yet

---

* Stott's parentheses.

running from God, as the moment of conversion is upon them. There must be a resolving of this ambivalence before conversion can be said to have taken place. The potential convert has to feel somehow that he and God are no longer competitors or enemies trying to win a power struggle in the person's life. John Knox helps clarify what is happening in the resolution of this conflict. He reminds us of Alfred North Whitehead's belief that religion runs through three stages if it evolves to its final satisfaction. It is the transition from *God the void* to *God the enemy*, and from *God the enemy* to *God the companion*.[4]

What is meant by *God the companion?* Knox suggests that this stage, when realized (or to the extent it is realized), means a free and inward capitulation to the "enemy," an allowing of ourselves to be captured by the God who seeks us. This stage is the "final satisfaction" because we discover in the moment of surrender that the God who is on our trail is also the God we seek. In a strange manner, as we seem to be defeated, it dawns on us that we are, in the only possible way, *victorious!* For we are free from having to run from God (who is everywhere), and we can turn and embrace him.

Our semiconscious fear of surrendering and being totally vulnerable is in that instant transformed into awe and relief. For we realize that God stood firm when we tried so frantically to push him away—not so he could destroy us or "control" us but in order to love us and help us find happiness. It is one of the most amazing surprises of the human pilgrimage.

As to what sort of response a person might make as he surrenders in the battle for the "God position" in his life, there are thousands of accounts. One classic statement is by Thomas à Kempis from the thirteenth century: "O Lord, all things that are in heaven and earth are thine. I desire to offer myself unto Thee, willingly and freely to be Thine forever . . . in the simplicity of my heart I offer myself unto Thee this day. . . ."[5]

A more contemporary statement might be this paraphrase of a nineteenth-century Christian's prayer of commitment: "Here, Lord, I abandon myself to you. I have tried in every way I could think of to manage myself, and to make myself what I thought I ought to be, but have always failed. Now I give it up to you. I give you permission to take entire possession of me."[6]

In many cases the response is not in words but is described as being dramatic but nonverbal: ". . . faith is here not so much believing this thing or that thing about God as it is hearing a voice that says, 'come unto me.' We hear the voice, and then we start to go without really knowing what to believe either about the voice or about ourselves; and yet we go. Faith is standing in the darkness and a hand is there, and we take it."[7] Or imagine the pilgrim emotionally exhausted, isolated from himself and others through having tried to "re-create the world" to satisfy his own needs. From the darkness of his own mind he reaches out toward that which he thinks may be God. Sometimes at that moment people have spoken of a wave of light breaking into their darkness. It is as though a voice were saying through the light, "You are accepted. You are accepted, accepted by that which is greater than you. . . ."*

The language difficulties in trying to describe a profound conversion experience are enormous. I think Goethe may have been close to the mark when he said that the greatest truths can only be expressed dramatically. (God seems to have felt the same way in presenting the truth about himself in the Scriptures.) Perhaps only those who have been down this road to the point of surrender can easily recognize the landmarks and the language of response.

But whether the act of surrender is verbal or nonverbal, the subjective *experience* that follows is often a glorious one of *re-*

---

* See Paul Tillich, *The Shaking of the Foundations* (London: S.C.M. Press, 1949).

ceiving from God. It is like being released from an intense and frightening struggle for one's very life. For some people, that which is received is a great release from guilt, a sense of forgiveness and new relatedness. Others have gained a personal revelation of meaning to life. Some feel that they have been given the security, love, or esteem they have worked so hard for. Still others receive personal power, or perhaps a deep intuitive realization that at last they have the freedom to begin to become the self they vaguely dreamed possible—living in a less bound and more loving and creative way. But in almost every instance, that which is received seems in some inexplicable way to relate to the satisfying of the frantic needs one had tried so desperately to meet on his own. And the convert sees his world with different eyes.

With a new perspective often comes a great wave of love for God and more particularly for Jesus Christ. There is a sense of loyalty and sometimes of being filled with the same spirit which was in Christ.*

As one "experiences" the gospel message in conversion, many of the basic questions about life are laid to rest. Is reality evil or gracious? Conversion indicates that it is gracious to the point of insane generosity. Is life meaningless or does it have a purpose? The new convert hears the reply of Jesus that not only does life have purpose but God has directly intervened in human events to convey the meaning of that purpose. What is the nature of the Really Real? Jesus' response is that the Really Real is generous, forgiving, saving love. In the end, will life triumph over death or death over life? The new follower of Jesus Christ is perfectly confident: God's Kingdom cannot be vanquished, not even by death.

---

* All converted Christians do not of course have the same sequence of events and feelings. For instance, some have a separate experience later in which they feel the overwhelming love of Jesus and the "filling" of their lives with his Holy Spirit.

Jesus is saying that in the end it will be all right, that nothing can hurt us permanently, that no suffering is irrevocable, that no loss is lasting, that no defeat is more than transitory, that no disappointment is conclusive.* And newly converted Christians tend to "know" these things are true, even though it may be years before they are able to articulate convincing reasons . . . if ever.

* See Andrew M. Greeley, *The Jesus Myth* (New York: Doubleday, 1971), pp. 48, 49, for an elaboration of these ideas.

CHAPTER THREE

❖

CONSCIOUS CONTACT
WITH GOD
—PRAYER

MEMORANDUM

TO: Keith

FROM: Bruce

RE: Chapter 3, Conscious Contact With God—Prayer

After conversion, I suppose the first important change inside my life was the stark realization that from *now on* I was going to be present to God in *my* mind as well as his.

When we talked about this I remember your saying something like: "If commitment means consciously entering a right relationship with God, then prayer has got to be the language of that relationship."

How did you begin to pray *after* conversion? (Because I know you prayed sometimes before too.) If God is "in his Heaven" and knows our thoughts already, why pray and tell him again? And what kind of prayer do you think gets "results"?

B.

❖ Aᴌᴌ ᴏꜰ ᴍʏ ʟɪꜰᴇ ɪ ʜᴀᴠᴇ ʙᴇᴇɴ ʟᴏᴏᴋɪɴɢ ꜰᴏʀ a sense of completeness in my soul. I have done a great deal of nervous talking about what I would like to do with my life. And I have sent up dozens if not hundreds of urgent prayers for guidance. I have studied. I have competed in business and socially. I have jumped in and espoused safe causes in the church. But all of my turning from one thing to another, my fantastic searching, had left me exhausted and afraid that there was no peace, no real continuity of purpose and direction for a person in his or her soul.

And then it had come . . . the falling into place of the key piece of the puzzle—not intellectually, but intuitively. How can one describe this integrating conformation of meaning to life, this release from that many-headed monster: the fear of unfulfillment, hiding somewhere in the darkness ahead?

When I was a small boy we lived in a two-story house near the edge of town. One day I was playing alone in my parents' bedroom upstairs. I was sitting on the floor, completely absorbed, playing with some toy soldiers, a brass tray, and a large battered tablespoon, among other things. Suddenly I looked up and realized I was totally alone in the house. I remember the throbbing silence. The aloneness terrified me and I began to sing and beat on the brass tray with the battered tablespoon, somehow feeling that if I could only keep up the noise nothing would creep up and get me. I remember being afraid to shout "Mother" for fear it (whatever it was that was going to get me) might know I was frightened and come out of its hiding place. The terror was agony; and I remember singing at the top of my lungs and beating the brass tray with huge tears streaming down my face and my heart about to jump out of my chest. When at last my mother came in from the backyard and came upstairs, I can still remember the feeling of exhaustion and the tears of relief as I collapsed into her arms and was released from my self-made prison of noise and fear.

I think something that "felt" like this took place in that first attempt to surrender my will to God by the roadside. But it was *more* than emotion. Martin Buber has tried to describe what happens to people when they encounter God personally. He says, "Man receives and he receives not a 'specific content' but a Presence, a Presence as power."[1] He is bound up in a new relation. Now this is no lightheaded release from the responsibility of intelligent thought "nor does it in any way lighten his life—it makes his life heavier, but heavy with meaning . . . there is the inexpressible conformation of meaning. Meaning is assured. Nothing can any longer be meaningless. The question about the meaning of life is no longer there. But were it there, it would not have to be answered. You do not know how to exhibit and define the meaning of life, you have no formula nor picture for it, and yet it has more certitude for you than the perception of your senses."[2] This was true for me as I set out to try to live my life for Jesus Christ.

But one of the first things I came to realize was that I didn't know how to begin to find God's will for me particularly. I had always rather naïvely assumed that the making of a "total commitment" sort of automatically ushered into one's experience a vital prayer life (whatever that meant) and ushered out the preoccupation with old resentments, fears, or thoughts of sleeping with someone other than one's wife. But this was not the case for me.

I have always pictured my inner life as a sort of cavern inside my head out of which I look at you, the rest of the world, through my eyes in the wall of the cavern. This cavern has a pool of liquid filling it about two-thirds full. The part above the surface of the pool is my conscious life and the larger part, beneath the surface where I cannot see, is my unconscious life. The day I decided to commit my life wholly to God, I scooped up everything I could see above the level of consciousness and offered it to Christ. I felt free; but then, several mornings later a hoary head came up out of the slimy pool, an old resentment.

I was filled with discouragement and I thought I must not have really committed my life to God at all. But then I realized joyously that of course I had—that all we do when we commit our "whole life" is to commit that of which we are conscious. And according to many psychologists, the major part of the human psyche is below the level of consciousness.[3] So the totally "committed" Christian life is a life of continually committing one's self and problems day by day as they are slowly revealed to his or her own consciousness. I think many Christians have become discouraged or given up because they have at some time made a new beginning with God and then found their minds filled with lust, resentment, and jealousy. Discouraged, they have assumed that they are not in right relationship with God at all. Naturally they do not want to admit these problems in their Sunday school classes, since they assume the rest of us are not plagued with such horrible and unchristian thoughts.

But since I now wanted to commit my future to God, I had to find out *specific* ways to align my rebellious and wavering will to his. I had always "prayed" sporadically; but my prayer life was a rather mechanical monologue. I had prayed about *big* things (cancer, success, deliverance) but didn't want to disturb God over the *little* problems of everyday living (resentment, jealousy, slothfulness). Now suddenly I realized that there are no small decisions—since every deciding either takes one closer to or further from God's will.

In order to develop a fulfilling prayer life, I had tried books of prayer, reading Psalms, and all sorts of devotional books. But again and again I wound up praying something like: "Dear God, forgive me for all the bad things I do. Help me to be better; thank you for all the many blessings you have given me; and help everybody everywhere." That prayer seemed to pretty well cover everything, but nothing much *happened* in my life. Then people began to tell me I needed to have a certain period of time each day for private prayer. I tried that . . . and failed, over and over, to get up that few minutes before everyone else did in the mornings.

I can remember the alarm going off those mornings (very early). I would wake up and force myself to my feet to feel around in the dark for my robe and slippers in the closet or for my Bible in the blackness. If I couldn't find everything right away, I would tell God sleepily, "Lord, you know it is not fair for me to wake up my family (who need their sleep) just to satisfy my selfish desire to have a time of prayer. Deliver me from that kind of legalism." And I'd go back to bed.

Or I can remember waking up early on cold winter mornings after a late night up and saying, "Lord, you know how unreasonable I am with my family when I don't get enough sleep. And since you have made it clear to me recently that I should be more thoughtful of them, I'm going to sleep this morning . . . knowing . . . you will . . . understand."

Or I can remember other times when I have awakened and decided to pray in bed in that semi-drowsy, half-conscious state (when the will is disengaged). These times certainly felt "spiritual," but they are not, I learned, to be substituted for the total life of prayer.

Nothing seemed to be working and I knew there was something really missing in my prayer life. Finally one day I met a layman whose life had a power and a concern in it which I knew instinctively were the things my Christian life desperately lacked.

Everywhere this man went he left in his wake men and women who began to be different people and whose lives became disciplined and focused on the Living God. I asked this man what he considered to be most important in the development of his Christian life. He pointed out that reading the Scriptures every day and having a specific time of prayer for the cultivation of a real and dynamic relationship with Christ were the two things that had become most meaningful and real to him.

Seeing a *life* with which I could identify did for me what all my "trying" could not—motivated me to begin a regular time of prayer and devotional reading of the Bible each day. I began, and through faith in another man's faith, was able to continue through the dry periods until now this time has become the center from which I live the rest of my life.

At this point things began to change. I realized that if Christianity is a living relationship with God I had to find out what this God is really like to whom I had committed my future. I realized that my closest relationships had always been with those who knew the most about me, and loved me anyway. So I began to reveal my inner life to God, all of it (even though I knew he already knew). This experience taught me the strange power in prayer of being *specific* with God. After making as total and complete a confession of all of the moral weaknesses and specific sins I could recall, I thanked him for his forgiveness. I began to examine myself daily and "keep short accounts with God."

In trying to be totally honest I found a new freedom and sense of being accepted. For now I didn't psychologically need to gloss over my true greed and resentments and excuse them as being insignificant. I knew I was accepted. Instead of saying, "Lord, today I exaggerated a little on my expense account, but you know everyone does." I was able to say, "Lord, I *cheated* on my expense account today. Help me not to be a dirty thief. Forgive me and give me the power and the desire to be different."

As I read passages like 1 John 1:9, I began to really believe that God could forgive me and would. And my desires began to change. Things began to be different not only in my devotional time but in my whole day. In looking for *specific* things to thank God for each morning I began to see his hand everywhere, and life became richer and filled with good things.

For a long time I had been disturbed about the problem of a wandering mind during my time of prayer. I would be trying to pray and suddenly my mind would jump to a business appointment I needed to make. For years I had forced these things out of my mind to get back to "spiritual things." But now, thanks to another Christian friend, Donn Moomaw, I began to keep a notebook by my side; and when the thought came to me to call someone, to make an appointment, or to do something for the family, I began to jot it down and then go back to God. I was at last realizing that he is interested in my total life and that these things which came into my mind during my time of prayer might be significant things for me to do, or places for me to go. This also made it easier for me to get my mind immediately back to my other prayers.

Sometimes a vision of someone I resented would come floating into my prayers or some incongruous situation that I did not want to think about. Instead of suppressing it, I began to offer the person or the thing immediately to God in prayer, asking him to make my thoughts about this person more like his. I began to keep a list of people for whom I wanted to pray. And before I knew it, I discovered that God was touching more and more of my life through this time of prayer. I realized experimentally that the Incarnation means that God has made the material world of people and things his concern and that we must make it our concern for him.

But there was a fly in the ointment. I found that although I had believed God could forgive me for all my selfishness and sins, I discovered that I could not forgive myself for one of them in particular. After months of inner anguish and continued confusion I was talking to a close Christian friend. In a prayer I confessed this sin aloud to God before this friend. And within a few days, I could accept God's forgiveness. As a Protestant I had always been repelled (and frightened) at the idea of revealing my true self before another person. But now I realized why Luther made the admonition in James to "confess your sins to one another" (James 5:16) a part of the Priesthood of all believers.[4]

This experience opened a whole area of my Christian life. I realized that once a person has confessed sins to God *before another person*, he or she can never again pretend (comfortably) to be righteous . . . however famous he or she may become as a Christian personality. There is no point in expanding time and energy on trying to impress others about how good we are because at least one other fallible human being—the one who heard our confession—knows better. I am not recommending this to anyone. I am merely saying that *I* was trapped with some terrible anguish; and through this kind of specific confessing with a trusted friend (who I knew might fail me), I found myself in a position in which I had to trust God with my reputation . . . and I found a new freedom. I could begin to be my true self with other people, realizing that as awful as I am, Christ loved me enough to die for me and people like me. Now I really *wanted* to be different in my life *out of gratitude*.

At this point a new honesty crept into my prayers. Before this, I had always started out by saying, "God, I adore you" (whether I really did or not that morning). Now I could say (when it was true), "Lord, I am sorry but I am tired of you today. I am tired of trying to do your will all of the time, and I'd like to run away and raise hell." But now I could also continue, "But, Lord, forgive me for this willfulness, and even though I don't 'feel like it', I ask you to lead me today to be your person and to do your will." This was a real act of *faith*, because there was no religious feeling involved. My days began to take on the character of adventure.

Howard Butt, Jr., has been a tremendous help to me at this point. He once told me about waking up one morning and beginning a time of prayer only to find that he was as stale and flat as he could be. He couldn't sense God's Presence at all. But he said, "God, I thank you for being with me even though I don't *feel* as if you are within a thousand miles." When he said this, I at once thought it sounded like some kind of autosuggestion; but he continued and said, "Lord, I believe you are here, not because I feel like it, but I believe it on faith in the authority of your Word. You said you would be with us." As he continued I realized that in so much of my life I had been a spiritual sensualist, always wanting to *feel* God's presence in my prayers and being depressed when I didn't. I saw that until I could believe *without* spiritual goose pimples I would always be vacillating, and my faith would be at the mercy of my emotional feelings. So I tried this praying whether I felt spiritual or not; and for the first time in my life found that we *can* sometimes live on raw faith. I found that often the very act of praying this way brings later a closer sense of God's Presence. And I realized a strange thing: if a person in his praying has the *feeling*, he doesn't really need the *faith*. I began to feel very tender toward God on those mornings during which I would pray without any conscious sense of his Presence. I felt this way because at last I was giving back to him the gift of faith.

Things began to change more rapidly in my inner life. It wasn't that I got rid of all my problems (as many Christian witnesses and evangelists seem to imply, thus making us all feel guilty and inadequate when we have problems). But I simply began getting a *new set* of problems. I came to realize that God wasn't going to take things out of my life. Instead he *brought* in a great many positive new things. Since my life and my time were already filled to overflowing, some things had to go . . . but he made *me* choose what they would be. And it was a great day when I found my whole set of values and my honest secret inner desires were changing. In a life of faith, I discovered, "renunciation is not sacrifice."[5] I had read and now saw the truth in the late Mahatma Gandhi's statement: "Only give up a thing when you want some other condition so much that the thing has no longer any attraction for you, *or* when it seems to interfere with that which is more greatly desired."[6] At first I had thought that if this were true I was stuck with some of my problems for life. But now I found that this advice was actually becoming true in my own prayer life. I began to *want* to be Christ's person enough to pray that he would reveal to me those thoughts and habits which were standing between him and me and my doing his will. I prayed that he would then give me the desire and the power to change.

Right here I ran into a problem that is very subtle even among the ranks of the newly committed disciples of our Lord. That problem was this: for years I had been engaged in a conformity to the social and economic world. This conformity had influenced the kind of clothes I wore and the kind of house I lived in, etc. But now having recognized this conformity to the world, I was tempted to trade it (unconsciously) for a conformity with the prevailing opinions of my new Christian friends concerning my behavior. In other words, as I prayed that God would reveal any changes I should make in my life, I was at the same time being pressured from the outside to make changes by Christian friends who were slightly appalled at some of my activities as a "good Christian." I am convinced that the changing of my behavior for reasons other than that of honestly believing that *Christ* would have me change it leaves the door open to all kinds of cliquish spiritual pride and self-righteousness (regardless of whether or not the change itself is good).

But how does one actually go about deciding to change his or her social and ethical behavior as a committed Christian? And having decided, how does one carry out these changes without being a pious fraud? Several years ago I might have thought that these questions were out of place in a discussion on a life of prayer. But if a Christian life is one of praise and adoration and the conforming of one's life and world to the purposes and will of God, then I realized that a life of prayer to have any fiber or reality about it had better also deal with the areas yet unchanged.

One of the things God brought into my already full life as a young businessman was the desire to tell other people that life wasn't a hopeless rat race, to tell them the Good News. This led to my beginning to teach an adult Sunday school class. Because many of the members of this class were college professors with advanced degrees, my intense pride demanded a great deal of study and preparation for Sunday morning. As I began to study about ten hours a week for my thirty-minute talk on Sunday morning, several things began to demand change.

We had often stayed out late on Saturday nights, going to dinners, movies, dances . . . mostly involving some preparatory social drinking, some sustaining social drinking and/or some later "one for the road" social drinking. But as I began to go home and try to put the finishing touches on my Sunday school lesson at

2:30 A.M. some Sunday mornings, I realized that, just as a practical matter if nothing else, some changes were in order. So we started coming in earlier. When we began to reserve Sunday as a family day with the children, we found that we felt terrible physically after a late evening with too much to eat or drink. I discovered that in order to be a loving parent and thoughtful husband (which I now really wanted to be) I needed more sleep than I was getting anyway. So I began to *want* to live a life with more order and moderation in it enough to see how we could have one. And the subsequent changes in our social life opened a whole new world of personal relationships and family activities I had never before "had time for."

All this time, while I was praying for God to reveal his will to me, I was being confronted in my soul with relationships that needed changing, attitudes toward my family, my work, minority groups, sexual lust, the magazines I was reading, my lack of involvement in politics as a Christian, and a good many other things that brought me to my knees continually in frustration mixed with the joy of knowing that God was changing my perspective and desires. He was giving me the power to occasionally be at least intellectually the free man I had always wanted to be in these areas.

As I continued to pray and read the New Testament, I learned that Christ's criteria for a godly life were not doctrinal as ours so often are. His had to do with allegiance to himself and the *fruits* that allegiance produced in a person's *relationships with other persons* (John 1:12, NEB; Matthew 7:15 f.; 11:2 f.; 12:33; 25:31 ff.; Luke 10:29–37, etc.). And I began to see that a life of prayer is to be judged ultimately not so much by even our devotion in praying and witnessing and inner moral rectitude as by whether or not we have fed the hungry, clothed the naked, and loved the loveless stranger (Matthew 25:31 f.). It dawned on me with a sudden jolt that real prayer, Christian prayer, inevitably drives a person, sooner or later, out of the privacy of his or her soul, beyond the circle of Christian friends and *across the barriers between social, racial, and economic strata to find the wholeness, the real closeness of Christ in that involvement with the lives of his lost and groping children whoever and wherever they may be.*

But behind and woven through all of these outer problems and adjustments a new inner prayer life had developed. There was a sense of active adventure. My prayers were no longer vague, mystical "feelings." I was communicating with a God who was alive, about real issues and real people in my days and nights. I was thanking him and offering him praise. God was trying to give me an abundant new experience of life, when and if I would take it . . . a day, an hour at a time. When my regular morning prayers would start out "dry" I learned to read devotional books (like *My Utmost for His Highest* by Oswald Chambers or *The Imitation of Christ* by Thomas à Kempis) to turn my thoughts toward him, toward Christ. Then I had found that by following any such reading with a passage from the New Testament every day I was gradually filling my unconscious life with God's message. And as I was revealing myself to him in confession, he was revealing his character and purposes to me through the reading again of the way Christ reacted throughout the story of his life, death, and resurrection and of his spirit in the formation and development of the early church.

I began to see as I never had the relationship of my prayer life to my physical and emotional life. A large glass of hot water and a few minutes of regular exercises just before one's prayer time each morning can change the whole climate of one's relationship with God and with other people. Because we are to come to him with our whole lives . . . not just our "spirit."

I have begun to learn to love Christ personally. For now we

have been through years of struggles and failures and joys together in the privacy of my soul and on the outer stage of my life. I have come to want to find new ways to praise him for giving me a sense of forgiveness, of unity, of wholeness, in my life. All of the different personalities I had projected in the various areas of my experience were somehow being melded into one. I didn't have to have a separate vocabulary, a different kind of humor and different set of ethics for my business life, my church life, my family life, and my prayer life. It was as if Christ had taken his fist and begun to knock out the partitions in my soul which had made my life so fragmented.

Finally, I began to see that prayer is not a series of requests to get God to help me do things I think need to be done. Prayer for me is a direction of life, a focusing of one's most personal and deepest attention Godward. The purpose is to love God and learn to know him so well, that our wills, our actions will be more and more aligned with his, until even our unconscious reactions and purposes will have the mark of his love, his life about them. Prayer was no longer an "activity." It had become the continuing language of that relationship God designed to fulfill a human life.

MEMORANDUM

TO: Bruce

FROM: Keith

RE: Chapter 3, Conscious Contact With God—Prayer

I'm not really satisfied with my part of the chapter on prayer. Will you try to write about your experience with prayer as conversation and lay down some specific guidelines? I get so enamored with the drama in my experience that I keep needing you to put some structure and form into the "whats" and "hows."

You know what I mean: things like how, when, and where these conversations can take place. And not only what kind of things do you find it helpful to pray about, but what should our attitudes be and how should we respond to any guidance received from God?

K.

❖ JESUS ONCE MADE THE STATEMENT: "WHAT-
ever you ask in my name, I will do it." I wonder how many praying
people really believe this? Sometimes I have found myself praying
with the same faith one usually has in a slot machine. "It won't
cost too much, and I might hit the jackpot."

I am convinced that most of us Christians really want to know
how to pray. We want to discover the power of God, which is
rightfully ours in Jesus Christ.

Prayer it seems to me is conversation between two persons. Of
course conversation in itself is neither good nor bad. We all know
what it is like to talk to The Gossip, The Bore, or The Crank.
Such conversation is not helpful and at times is really harmful.
Then there is the conversation that you have with the man who
comes to read your water meter which is neither helpful nor
harmful but polite and routine. Conversation is what you make
it. It can be irrelevant, or as crucial as a midnight phone call to
the doctor. It can be dull or stimulating. It can be necessary and
businesslike or it can lead to deep relationships or even marriage.

In the same way prayer can be as meaningless as much of our
conversation, or it can be conversation between you and God
that is vital, exciting, and transforming.

Conversation always implies some kind of a relationship between two or more persons. The quality of the conversation
depends on the kind of relationship that exists between the two.

I believe our prayers as Christians should be intimate conversations with God, because through Jesus Christ we become children and God becomes a loving Father. And yet, how many
times we wake up every morning, meet God at the breakfast
table, and say some little jingle that rhymes to thank him for the
food. If I spoke that way to my wife every morning, it would be
grounds for divorce. It would be an insult to speak that way to an
intelligent person.

Yet we believe that God, though he is a Spirit, is a Person. Why talk to him as though he were a statue or a simpleminded child? This is why Jesus warns us, "Do not use vain repetitions (or empty phrases) as the heathen do; for they think that they will be heard for their many words." We deny God is our Father when we talk to him only in memorized prayers or little singsong jingles. A child's first words to his earthly parents are not a singsong jingle, but a meaningful word or two conveying an honest request. Why should this not apply when speaking to one's heavenly Parent? When a child is old enough to be taught to pray, he is old enough to learn that prayer is personal conversation with a heavenly Father.

What does Jesus mean when he says, "Whatever you ask in my name, I will do it . . . "? It seems obvious that he does not mean to pray using his name as a sign-off at the end of a prayer, but rather to pray in his name by experiencing him as Lord and Savior and through him to experience God as Father. Believing that God exists is not the same as experiencing him as Father. To experience him as Father is to enter into a new relationship with him—Person-to-person—and to grow daily in this relationship.

I would say that the most important single factor in effective prayer is that the person praying be in the right relationship with God.

Guideposts for Effective Prayer

Once you are in the right relationship with God, the following guideposts may prove helpful in making your prayer life more effective:

With Whom Should I Pray? Part of your prayer life should include prayer alone with God. Jesus said, "When you pray, go into your room and shut the door and pray to your Father who is in secret." Part of your prayer life should be with others. Jesus said, "If two of you agree on earth about anything they ask, it will be done for them by my Father in heaven. For where two or three are gathered in my name, there am I in the midst of them." Families need to pray together. This helps immeasurably in enabling our children to learn to pray.

When Should I Pray? I pray in the morning, trying to give God my day and my troubles and put myself at his disposal for service. I also pray in the evening. It helps me to take an inventory of my day and then ask forgiveness where I have failed and thank him where he gave me power to overcome. As a matter of fact I find it helpful to pray at times all day long—while working or walking or talking with others. Learn to pray short sentences all day long that ask for help or give thanks. Let God know that you know that he is there.

In What Position Should I Pray? Pray in any position throughout the day. The main thing is that you pray. The position is not important. I have one friend who talks with God while driving to work in the morning. He imagines that God is sitting on the seat next to him and they talk about plans for the day.

Listen When You Pray. At least half of good conversation ought to be listening. Most of us seem to ask God for advice and guidance and then never listen for an answer. I try to spend half of my prayer time in quiet listening. Learn to expect answers. Believe that God really wants to talk to you.

Respond Immediately to Guidance. Respond immediately to whatever guidance God gives you in prayer. Until you walk in the light of what you have, I'm convinced you will never get more light. God's guidance could be compared to the light on a miner's hat which throws a beam six feet ahead. Unless you walk those six feet, you will never see more of the path before you. So God's guidance is step by step.

Be Positive When You Pray. Be positive when you pray, especially when praying for someone who is sick. Have a picture in your mind of that person already made well and whole and ask God to accomplish just that. This is where faith comes in. I do not believe in praying with a negative attitude where you cry out to God to prevent the worst from happening (and hence picture that person at his worst in your mind while you pray). Rather, faith for me is believing God will heal and has already healed through the presence and power of Christ, even while you pray.

Pray Believing. Jesus says, "Therefore I tell you, whatever you ask in prayer, believe that you receive it and you will." That's how faith is experienced. It is belief in the love and power of God to act. Jesus says in another place, "Whatever you ask in prayer, you will receive if you have faith."

Relax. Relax, both physically and spiritually, when you pray. One man says, "Don't pray hard. Pray easy. Prayer doesn't do it. God does it." Relaxed prayer takes a lot of faith for me. Faith is evidently demonstrated by our trust. And trust shows clearly in our relaxation. I've found a good technique to follow is to pray with your palms open and turned up, not with your fingers clenched together. Lift people and situations and yourself to God for help on your open palms.

Surrender. Surrender when you pray. Don't merely ask God

for help. Give situations and people to God and trust him. This is sometimes impossible but I think it underlies all prayer and may be the most important single guidepost to remember. It is not enough to believe that God loves us and can help us. We must so trust him that we let go of things and give them to him.

There is a young mother I know whose little boy of five came down with meningitis. She stayed by his bed in the hospital, helping the nurses and praying constantly, but his fever of 106° continued. After more than thirty hours a nurse shared some distressing news. He should have responded to the medication in five to eight hours. She implied that there was no hope. With this, the mother got to her knees and surrendered the child to God, whom she knew loved him even more than she did. As his pain was unbearable, she put Bobby in God's hands and asked him for quick death or quick recovery, believing that this was what a loving Father would want for his child. As she surrendered him to God's love, peace came to her instantly. But that is not all. Within the hour the boy's fever broke and healing came.

If you believe these three simple facts when you pray, I think you can expect miracles:

1. Believe that Christ loves you even more than you love yourself. The cross is evidence of this. (Read John 15:13.)

2. Believe that all power is his, physically as well as spiritually. (Read Matthew 28:18.)

3. Believe that he is right there with you when you pray. (Read Matthew 28:20.)

Build your prayers on these facts, and then your Lord may say to you, "Whatever you ask in my name, I will do it."

CHAPTER FOUR

❖

THE BIBLE

MEMORANDUM

TO: Bruce

FROM: Keith

RE: Chapter 4, The Bible

As I recall our conversations about those things which became important to us in the beginning, we decided to move from the inside out, dealing first with the more intimate and personal aspects of the Christian life as we have experienced it, and moving gradually outward toward the people and institutions around us.

For me, after (or during) prayer came a need to know all I could about this Jesus Christ I'd thrown in my lot with. People told me I should "read the Bible" to find out more about God and his will. I had studied the Scriptures in seminary, but I'd never "listened to God" through reading the words.

Since the Bible has become so important in both our lives, Bruce, I'm for doing what you suggested and each one writing what he thinks the Bible is and does and what it basically says. Since neither of us has ever sat down to do this specifically, I'll be interested to see what we come up with.

In the last chapter on prayer in your "guideposts" you emphasized the need for serious listening and responding to God's will as we can determine it. How about starting now by dealing with some questions like, What does the Bible have to do with our ongoing prayer life? What *is* the Bible anyway? And are there specific questions or guidelines an untrained layperson can bring to a biblical passage to help grasp its meaning for living?

K.

❖ IF BEING A CHRISTIAN CENTERS ON RELA-
tionships with God and people, then it was apparent to me from
the beginning that communication was going to be the main
problem.

Someone once said that the Kingdom of God is the kingdom
of right relationships. And to be in a right relationship with God,
one must be able to communicate with him—able to speak with
assurance *and* to hear what he says in return. As a new Christian
I began to try to be more real in my conversations with God, but
I soon found out I needed to learn more about Christ before I
could have any sound basis for knowing if what I "heard" in my
prayers was from God or only from my unconscious life. So I
began to read the Scriptures in a more "listening and receptive"
way. And this reading gave me a lot more confidence in attempting to respond to God.

But of course this raised the whole question of "What is the
Bible?" and "How did it get to be important and trustworthy
enough to risk letting its message change one's behavior—and
perhaps ruin his life?"

At Oxford, England, two bishops were burned at the stake
because of their efforts to make the Bible available to ordinary
people in their own language. A crowd had gathered to watch the
execution of Hugh Lattimer and Nicholas Ridly. And surely one
of history's most dramatic moments occurred as the fires were lit.
"Be strong, Master Ridly," called Lattimer to his fellow martyr.
"Play the man; for today we will light such a candle as by the
grace of God will never go out."

We cannot help but ask ourselves what there is about the Bible
that inspired people to lay down their lives with this kind of
abandon. In parts of the world this very day people are suffering
all kinds of hardships and deprivations to translate the Bible into
dialects and languages where it still is not known.

To begin with, the Bible is a unique Book unlike any other book that ever was written or ever could be written. The Hebrew Christian traditions from the Bible are the basis for European and American culture and for much of Western civilization in general. The Bible may have been the source and inspiration of more ideas, philosophy, ethics, literature, and art than all other books put together.

Now, certainly the above reasons would be sufficient to make reading the Bible important for everyone. But, for Christians, the Bible has an even more unique and different function. While I was at Princeton Seminary, our president, John Mackey, gave an inspired lecture that I will never forget about the Bible. He called it the Book of human destiny. According to John Mackey, the Bible tells man who he is, where he has come from, where he is going, and what life is meant to be.

We find an amazing illustration of this dimension of the Bible in the story of Pitcairn Island. Following the famous mutiny on the ship *Bounty*, Fletcher Christian and his men put Captain Bly and his loyal crew adrift. The *Bounty* sailed for Pitcairn Island, where the crew wrecked their boat and began to build a new life with the natives who were with them. Now, the island was a literal paradise. But the *Encyclopedia Britannica* tells us that they soon created a "hell on earth."

One of the sailors, who had previously worked in a distillery in Scotland, had discovered a way to make alcohol from one of the native plants, and drunkenness and violence resulted. Before long all the native men were dead and the only remaining white man was Alexander Smith. He was left alone with a harem of native women and a crowd of half-breed children, some of whom were his own.

Then something dramatic happened. Looking through some of the chests that had been salvaged from the *Bounty*, Alexander

Smith found a Bible. He opened it and began to read. In despair over what was to become of this tiny new settlement, he found the Bible gave him answers about his own destiny and the destiny of the people there.

Well, the years passed; the children grew up and married, and more children came and the community seemed to prosper. Many years later when the first ship landed on that island (the U.S. Navy's ship *Topaz*), they found a seemingly perfect civilization. There was no illiteracy, no crime, no disease, no mental illness. The island was 100 percent Christian. The *Britannica* states that nowhere on earth were life and property more safe than on Pitcairn Island.

Well, we have to ask ourselves how one Book could bring about such a transformation, not just in one man, but in a whole community and in succeeding generations. What exactly is in this Book that men like Lattimer and Ridly and a whole host of others gave their lives to make available?

The Bible has long been revered for its literature and poetry, but it is more than great literature or great poetry. As a history book it is incomplete, and skeptics point out historical inaccuracies and scientific incongruities. But you would not read a cookbook as a chemistry manual, or *Hamlet* as a history of Danish political development. In the same way, the Bible is not primarily a history book or a scientific manual.

And yet it is more than just a resource for our own private devotions or a handbook for theological controversy. It has been the source of two thousand years of sermons (good and bad). It is a great well of proof texts to back up any particular stand that a person wishes to take.

The critics of the Bible seem to feel that if they can find some flaw in dates or in geography or conflicting accounts of events they can then refute the whole Bible. But the Bible is not inerrant in some legalistic literary sense. Rather, it is infallible in what it claims to be. What it claims to be, very simply, is the Word of God; showing all men how to discover a life that is eternal and authentic. The basic Christian belief about the Bible then, is that it is not simply a collection of writings by religious, devout, or inspired men but is inspired by God and comes from him through men to us.

Listen to what John Wesley said about the authority of the Bible: "The Bible must be the invention either of good men or angels, bad men or demons, or God. (1) It could not be the invention of good men or angels because they would not make a book and tell lies all the time they were writing it, saying, 'Thus sayeth the Lord,' when it was their own invention. (2) It could not be the invention of bad men or demons, for they would not make a book which commands all duty, forbids all sin, and condemns their own souls to hell for all eternity. Therefore, draw the conclusion that the Bible must be given by the true and living God."

Now even this argument does not prove that the Bible is from God because that is beyond proof. But to read the Bible in faith is to begin with Wesley's assumption that it comes from God and is for our instruction.

The Bible was written in three primary languages by over forty authors during a period of one thousand years. That in itself is a mystery. How could the unity of theme—the redemption of humankind—be so infallibly and consistently presented over that long span of time through all those languages and cultures and through the thoughts and words of so many authors?

We find truth in the Bible and because we do, the Bible has often become an object for veneration and worship. I suspect that at times in my life I have been guilty of worshiping the Bible or the central fact of the Bible, which is reconciliation through Jesus

Christ, rather than worshiping the giver of the Bible, who is God. I always feel a bit uncomfortable when I see a sign proclaiming a Bible-centered church. Though the Bible is essential to an authentic faith, we are to be Christ-centered, not Bible-centered. And yet, most of what we know about God's plan for redemption and the history of his people from the beginning of recorded time comes from the Bible.

A shift in my own understanding of the Bible came when I realized that things are not true because they are in the Bible. Rather, things are in the Bible because they are true. And so I read the Bible mainly because I have come to know and love the author and because through it he reveals something about his love for me and his plan for me and for all people in any age.

Maybe the reason some people say they find the Bible dull is that they have no relationship with God and they're busy doing their own thing. But should they ever have an encounter with God and come to know him, immediately the Bible can become a meaningful book for them. That's why I am not enthusiastic about using Bible study as a means of evangelism. If we can instead introduce people to the living Christ as he gives us the opportunities, the Bible then becomes a book that the new child of faith wants to know and read.

As we become more serious students of the Bible it is easy to get deflected in all kinds of theological and historical controversies over which writer wrote which book at what time. Now these studies are tremendously important for theologians and we all benefit from the fruits of their years of study. I feel a real sense of gratitude that there are people who are doing this tedious and meticulous work for the rest of us. But I don't believe this is the vocation for the average believer.

I'm reminded of the story about a scientist who saw a workman in his building reading the Bible during his lunch break.

"What good is that going to do you?" asked the scientist. "You don't even know who wrote it."

The workman looked puzzled for a moment and then said, "It seems to me that you scientists working in this building make considerable use of the multiplication table in your calculations."

"Of course we do," said the scientist.

"Well, do you know who wrote it?"

"Why no, I guess I don't."

"So, how can you trust the multiplication table when you don't know who wrote it?" asked the workman.

"Well," the scientist said, "we trust it because . . . well, because it works."

"I read the Bible for the same reason," declared the workman. "It works."

I guess I read the Bible because it helps me make sense out of my senseless actions. Like Paul, the things that I would not I keep on doing and that which I would, I do not. The Bible gives me hope. It interprets my sin to me and deals with my guilt. It gives me an answer for my life. It tells me how to treat my brother and sister. It tells me who God is and how to love him. And that's why I read it.

Many people scoff at the Bible because they feel Christians claim it is infallible. The strange thing is that the Christian church historically has never believed in "an infallible Bible." All of the great reformers knew that there were errors in the Greek and Hebrew manuscripts in use during those first fourteen centuries of Christian history. They knew that there were no original manuscripts of the whole Book in existence. The historic Christian stance is that the Bible is infallible as "a rule of faith and practice," in its purpose of helping men to find the real God and to deal with their real problem, which is sin.

Well, let me now just suggest two ways that you and I can read the Bible. It can be tremendously important for many of us to know the setting of each of the books, to understand as best we can who wrote it, why it was written, to whom it was written, and under what circumstances. So I would strongly advocate that every serious Christian find commentaries, atlases, Bible dictionaries, concordances, and several translations (all the guides that he or she can get) and then try to find a good Bible teacher who can help him or her go through the Bible bit by bit, book by book to understand it in its original setting. This is one way to study the Bible.

But in addition to all that, you'll be missing something if you're not reading the Bible and letting God speak to you today in your condition as he understands you and your world. You can do this kind of study in your personal devotions or in a small group. I believe it is more helpful to read large chunks at one time . . . whole chapters rather than single verses. Or, possibly a whole book if it is a short one. But having read a whole unit of thought—a chapter or a number of chapters or a small book— here are four questions that can make such a study come alive.

1. What does this portion of Scripture tell me about God?
2. What does it tell me about human beings?
3. What is God saying to me in it about me and who I am?
4. What do I sense God is asking me to do now, today, because I read this?

New light is continually being shed upon the Bible through scholars, new translations, and rediscovered manuscripts. Yet the central truth remains unchanged. God is at work in Jesus Christ reconciling the world to himself. Because of this, I am convinced that the Bible will outlast the critics of every age.

I paused last eve beside the blacksmith's door,
And heard the anvil ring, the vespers chime,

And looking in I saw upon the floor
Old hammers, worn with beating years of time.

"How many anvils have you had?" said I,
"To wear and batter all these hammers so?"
"Just one," he answered. Then with twinkling eye:
"The anvil wears the hammers out, you know."

And so, I thought, the anvil of God's Word
For ages skeptic blows have beat upon,
But though the noise of falling blows was heard
The anvil is unchanged; the hammers gone.

John Clifford

MEMORANDUM

TO: Keith

FROM: Bruce

RE: Chapter 4, The Bible

Here's mine. From our conversation I assume you are going to take off at the point of how a new Christian might look at the Bible and then talk about the drama that ties the various parts of it together.

I hope you'll put in something about the main point you think God was trying to make throughout the story.

Also just as there are different experiences of conversion, I know there are different approaches to studying the Bible; and I think it would be good if you add what you've found there too (if you haven't already).

B.

❖ Wʜᴇɴ ɪ ʙᴇᴄᴀᴍᴇ ᴀ ᴄʜʀɪsᴛɪᴀɴ ɪ sᴏᴏɴ ᴅɪs-covered I was in for a lot of surprises. One of the first was that the Bible means very different things to different groups of Christians. Not only that, but each group or subgroup has its own preferred way to read or study the Scriptures. But all of the Christian denominations and groups I know about seem to agree on one basic point: the drama that makes up the Bible includes everything necessary for putting man in the right relationship with God (for "salvation"). The tragedy, it seems to me, is that beyond that basic common denominator certain groups think they have a corner on the "only way" to approach and interpret the Scriptures.

My own study and experience have led me to believe that the truth found in the library of books which make up what we call the Bible is much more divinely inspired than some of the more liberal textual critics think. And yet it is much closer to the guts and hearts of its very human writers than the absolute literalist would hold. In other words, to record his story God seems to have used *real* people with imperfect grammar and style and with varying motivations and commitments to God. And yet, the miracle is that through the guidance of his Holy Spirit the silver thread of God's story and people's perception of it is woven wholly into the fabric of the history and literature selected by God's people as their Holy Scriptures. The books chosen present the Good News that God loves us.

In order not to violate our freedom God presented himself to his people in different ways. And the story of the Bible is made up of the Hebrews' growing perception that God wanted to be their God and care for them. But the people kept choosing to use God to enhance their own will to power. Then tragedy. Then God would come to them again and forgive them and the cycle would start over.

In this recurring story the people are often dense, selfish, greedy, lustful, and power-mad. They misunderstand God, try to use him in all sorts of devious schemes for their own glory; and they foul up their lives and religious practices in almost every way imaginable. But God's continual willingness to begin again with them gradually allows them to see themselves and their sin. By the end of the Old Testament, they realize that "on their own" they cannot keep from fouling up their lives and getting out of a right relationship with God and people.

But throughout the Old Testament story there are hints that God will intervene in an even more dramatic and immediate way in their lives than by sending prophets and political leaders. They felt that God would someday send a unique representative to lead his people. This special one was to be God's own "anointed." To the Hebrew this meant "king" since their kings were anointed, beginning with Saul. The Hebrew word for "anointed one" we translate "Messiah." The Greek translation for the same word is *Christos* or "Christ." So the growing conviction of the ancient Hebrews was that God would send his own special king, anointed one, Messiah or Christ, who would somehow reveal God's own will and purposes for humankind. And this Messiah would come with the authority and power of God himself to allow the Hebrews to fulfill their destiny as his people.

Several different notions of what the Messiah would be like developed side by side. One group looked for a great king like David who would be the mighty and wise ruler of the nations and bring Israel back to political prominence. Another group thought God would send "the Son of man" who would come supernaturally on the "clouds of heaven" to establish God's reign. And a third strand of hope which developed alongside the other two was that God's special messenger would be one like a servant who would love his people enough to suffer deeply for them.

So when the New Testament part of the story—act two of the

drama—begins, Jesus of Nazareth has come onstage. And since he didn't exactly fit *any* of the preconceived pictures of the Messiah, the scholars and those in the religious power structures rejected him. But as Jesus' life and ministry progressed, the common people felt intuitively that he was God's man in a way other men were not. For Jesus spoke with great authority. He used the first person singular with a power few kings in history would have dreamed of. And everywhere he went men and women became whole. There was a miraculous healing in his words, his touch, his presence. And yet with all his striking moral and spiritual authority and the miraculous healing which surrounded his life and ministry, Jesus' language, his clothes, his vocation were of the common stuff of the earth and the ordinary man. And his approach to people was not from a stance of privilege and power. Rather, he approached people through serving them in meeting their needs for hope, meaning, worth, and healing. In his ministry he was exposed to the people without the protection of either wealth or position. He came to serve people and in his vulnerability he suffered.

Though he met no Jewish authority group's expectations, with his gifts he was gaining a strange kind of strong, motivating influence in people's lives. All of the existing power groups could agree on one thing—Jesus was a threat to their preconceptions and he had to go. So they got him crucified. And all his followers deserted him, believing that he had failed. But they and all the Jews had missed something.

Because in some mysterious way Jesus had fulfilled *all* the hopes of the seers of ancient Israel: he *did* speak with the clear authority of a king and demanded total allegiance to God. But he also was more than a "Son of man" in that there was a miraculous wholeness that communicated itself through his spirit even to the extent of healing people's bodies. And yet he was a suffering servant who came to live and die for the people.

On the third day after his death, according to the testimony of the New Testament authors, his followers saw him *alive* just as they did several other times after that day. And tradition tells us that the group of cowards who had deserted Jesus went out and turned the world upside down with their proclamation that God had indeed come to his people in a unique way. The Messiah, the Christ had come! And after his death, the same spirit they had seen in him they now saw and experienced in *each other*. And it was this Holy Spirit who would teach and guide them as they helped establish his Kingdom or reign, which they now realized was to be *within* people's hearts. And so, the New Testament, act two of the drama, ends with the beginning of the Christian church, which was really only another chapter in the same story of God's people.

Act three is the part of the drama *we* are living in. This part of the story began in one sense as the young Christians moved from Jerusalem to Rome and thus into the mainstream of history. Tradition reports that all of the apostles were martyred in painful ways, and yet evidently *not one* of these previously cowardly men denied what they had seen on the third day.

But the greatest evidence of the truth of the gospel story (which Christians believe to be the culmination of the whole Bible) is that the church *still exists*—that the spirit seen in the life of Jesus and then in the lives of the apostles and early Christians can be seen today, still healing men and women out of their brokenness and separation into right relationships with God, with each other, and with themselves.

It is this company of which we are a part, moving toward the *final* culmination of history, on which God through Christ will draw the curtains. And, in the meantime, ours are the power and freedom which can bring into the lives of other people great moral authority, healing presence, and vulnerable service to suffering humanity.

This is the Bible story in all its sweep and grandeur which also includes the songs, the wise sayings, the laws and moral precepts, the ancient visions of the beginnings of life. And the whole Bible reveals the faithfulness of God, and the seemingly incurable way-wardness of us in our freedom. In this great collection of words is God's Word or message to humankind.

How Does a Christian Approach the Bible—to Read It?

There may be more different opinions about the "best way" to read the Bible than there are notions about what it is. Some people say that the Bible should only be read with a commentary handy (and then only after having read a good survey introduction of the particular testament and book of the Bible being read). Others hold that since the Holy Spirit is the teacher, a Christian doesn't need any "helps" but should simply "read where he feels led to open the book."

But it seems to me that there are two basic reasons for reading the Bible, both essential to the life of Christians who want to work toward being mature in their faith.

One reason is to learn the background, the structure, and the content of the larger story which includes the gospel. This kind of learning can include a study of the origins of the various parts of the Bible, their authorship, dates, and the critical problems and contradictions found in various accounts. One can learn fascinating things about the differences in the concrete way the ancient Hebrews thought and expressed themselves as compared to the more abstract way we think and speak. We can learn things like the historical context out of which the various books were written and begin to understand the political and economic conditions that pressured the Israelites into forming a kingdom and developing it. And learning these kinds of overall structural facts makes the reading of any *specific* passage come alive with new and exciting richness.

A second basic reason for a Christian to read the Bible is for inspiration and learning how to live life as Christ's person. And although this kind of reading can be done in many different ways, it has been my experience and observation that some kind of regular reading in the Bible is a very important part of staying close to the God of Jesus Christ.

Since we are trying to uncover principles and approaches to help us *discover* and *live* God's will, it has been helpful to me to remember that Christians have always believed God's primary purposes and principles for living were *embodied* in the life, death, and resurrection of Jesus Christ. In him we have not only a teacher and a Savior but a walking, breathing case history of the Holy Spirit in action in relationships with the problems and joys of real life. So the reading of the New Testament lets us look through the eyes of many of the people who were trying to follow Jesus and give themselves to God—just as we are.

I'm not saying my way is best for anyone else, but I have found that *both* study *and* devotional reading have been necessary for me. I had taken a survey course in the Old and the New Testaments before I had made a conscious commitment to God. Later, I did a great deal of studying in connection with adult classes I taught at church. (When I really want to learn something I find that committing myself to *teach* it provides a fantastic motivation to *study* the subject in question.) But since many people cannot take survey courses on the Bible, there are some books that may be helpful.

It has been very useful to me to have a good Bible commentary to which I can refer when I hit a confusing passage. I also use a Bible dictionary which gives the definition and historical significance of many of the archaic words in the Bible. A Bible atlas has helped me to picture the Holy Land and to place the characters and events of the Bible story on a geographical stage at different periods of the Hebrews' history.

Some general sources that have helped me gain a background are: *The Drama of the Bible* by Theodore Wedel, *The Holy Scriptures* by Robert Dentan, *Understanding the Old Testament* by Bernard Anderson, *Old Testament Survey* by La Sor, Hubbard, and Bush, *Introducing the Old Testament* by John Drane, and *Understanding the New Testament* by Key and Young. The commentaries I use are *The Abingdon Bible Commentary* (in one volume) and *The Interpreter's Bible*, a twelve-volume commentary. Both are published by Abingdon Press. In the latter two categories mentioned above I have found *Harper's Bible Dictionary*, *Harper's Bible Commentary*, and the *Westminster Bible Atlas* to be very helpful.

Listing these books and suggesting that a Christian might do well to begin building his own simple reference library may make studying the Bible seem like a formidable task. But it really isn't. If a person has really committed his *life* to the finding and doing of God's will, he will probably find that he is deeply motivated to learn all he can about this God and his story in which we Christians are to walk.

This does *not* mean, of course, that one can't learn a great deal about God and his faith without a library—not everyone is oriented toward "book learning." For the nonstudent, the devotional approach to the Bible may prove to be more relevant—particularly at first.

Nevertheless, one should realize that he will be missing a great deal of the original meaning and context if he does not "study" too. Of course the truth is that *everyone* misses a lot of truth in the Bible, so no *scholar* can take his own interpretations *too* seriously.

For me the devotional reading of the Bible was very frustrating for years. I wanted to learn all I could about how to live for Christ, so I decided to begin reading about his life in the gospels—a chapter a day. Some days the material was relevant. But some days it seemed useless and a waste of time. I gave it up and started again—several times. But finally I met a Christian whose life was so real that I asked him what were the most important things he did to maintain his faith and grow in it.

He said that having a particular time every morning when he prayed and read the Scriptures was the most important thing he did for the inner part of his pilgrimage. I told him about my attempts and failures and my frustrations because "nothing seemed to be happening." He smiled and told me about his frustrations. "Then why do you keep doing it?" I asked.

He pointed out that since he had committed the *rest of his life* to trying to find and do God's will, he wasn't in such a frantic hurry to "grow." He said that it had occurred to him that he wanted to reprogram his entire life and perspective so that he could see and think as Christ did. If he could permeate his whole life—the conscious and unconscious parts of his mind—with the loving perspective of God, then his *natural reactions* might become loving and Christlike. Before that realization he had thought only in terms of his *conscious* life, but upon realizing that our minds are about two-thirds unconscious, he saw that something more than occasional conscious "study and memorizing" was necessary. To reach the unconscious, out of which come so many of our uncalled-for and consciously unwanted impulses, the only route to which we have access is through our consciously directed thoughts. So this man decided that he would begin each day by putting consciously into his mind a part of God's story, of his hopes and dreams for our lives. He wasn't going to worry about how "much he got out of it" for that day; but he was going to read as an athlete begins to get his whole body in condition, a short time every day. And so with faith in this man's faith, I began.

That was almost thirty-two years ago. And although I have no idea how much effect this habit of reading a chapter or two of the Scriptures each day during much of that time has had on my behavior, I am convinced that it has made my inner pilgrimage a much richer one. *

I have had lapses, sometimes long ones. But I keep coming back and beginning again. And the surprising thing has been how many times the subject that I am reading about on a given morning comes up *that same day* as a question, problem, or idea relating to a decision I must make. I have come to realize that this should not be surprising since most of the New Testament in particular was written to people who were struggling to understand what God did in Christ and how that related to living and communicating the Good News to other people. And since the authors were speaking out of their own experience to the experience of their fellow strugglers, they were speaking in many cases to me. And the "studying" aspect of my encounter with the Bible helped me to compare the specific similarities and *differences* of the problems and questions of the early Christians to my own.

Also, I have found that the process of reading the New Testament through (in one translation and then another) has affected the way I face and deal with questions that come to me. Often I do not even realize that I am responding with a "scriptural" response until later. What now seems like "common sense" sometimes later turns out to be something Jesus or Paul said.

No attempt to be comprehensive has been made in this brief

---

* Also for a period of some months I memorized a key verse of Scripture every day. This proved invaluable in giving me an index as to where certain aspects of the faith are discussed in the Bible.

and fragmented indication of *some* of the ways the Scriptures have been relevant and helpful to me. There are, of course, many other perspectives to investigate.

But what I am saying is that I have found through reading a chapter a day, thinking about what the author is saying, and asking myself if and how this material relates to my life, that this process has had a profound influence on my own experience of trying to learn to live as God's person.

❖

CHAPTER FIVE

RELATIONSHIP PRESSURES AND CHANGES BECAUSE OF CONTACT WITH GOD

MEMORANDUM

TO: Keith

FROM: Bruce

RE: Chapter 5, Relationship Pressures and Changes
Because of Contact With God

After going over the Bible chapter, I was trying to recall
some of the immediate effects reading the Scriptures and praying had in my life as a new Christian. I remember feeling that
I *should be* more loving (and feeling guilty because I wasn't—
except to people I liked and had things in common with already). Also I felt that I ought to be *doing* something
important to help the Kingdom to come faster.

Do you remember that morning about ten years ago when I
was driving you to the airport in New York and you were so
excited about realizing that you didn't have to do something
"big" for God? You were talking a hundred miles an hour
about ways you were just beginning to see people outside your
family and friends as *persons*—people you had never really noticed before.

I think you ought to bring those things in here. After you
began to get a conscious relationship with God going through
prayer and the Scriptures, what happened to your workday, for
instance? Can a person do his job well and still think about
being God's man or woman? How do you keep from day-
dreaming about being an outstanding Christian?

And then I wish you would talk some about what "Christian
love" of the people in your life means to you.

B.

❖ LIVING IN THE MOVING THICKET OF A COM-
muter's life, I guess I had been searching for a mighty plan to
mow down the seemingly unchristian complexity of the vocational jungle for Christ's sake. But I set out one morning to see
if I could learn to *live*, to simply be myself as God had made me.
I wanted to operate within my emotional income. This meant
that I would have to learn to live as an average, aggressive lay
businessman, walking along the insignificant paths on which my
own life in the city took me, day in and day out. I wanted to see
this life of mine as Christ saw his, walking along the paths he took
in Nazareth. I wanted to see my life from his perspective. If he
had not been bored with the commonplace things of life, who
was I to demand ever more exciting and scintillating companions, challenges, and experiences in order to be happy as a Christian. But I did not know how to begin living naturally. Finally I
decided to go through a whole day trying consciously to see what
I was *actually doing* to love the people with whom God had put
me. It was quite a day.

On the way to work I stopped for gasoline at the service station
I had been patronizing for several years. The attendant smiled
and said, "Good morning, Mr. Miller." I was sort of shocked as
I realized that I had seen this man dozens of times and yet had
never really noticed him as a *person*. He knew my name, and I
didn't have the vaguest idea what his was. And *I* was the Christian witness. I saw that this man might be a person to whom God
had introduced me to love for him. Glancing quickly at the name
tag on his uniform, I said, "Good morning, Charlie." After he
had serviced my car and I was signing the credit card receipt, I
tried to think of some natural thing to say to a man whom I had
ignored for three years to let him know I was interested in him as
a person. Because suddenly I *was*. I finally came out with, "Say,
Charlie, do you have a family?"

He stopped and looked at me a second. When he saw that I really seemed to want to know, his smile spread clear across his face. "Do I have a family?" And he pulled out his wallet with pictures of "about" nine children. This was the beginning of a new relationship that soon became a first-name friendship with Charlie. One of his kids later got seriously injured in an accident. When I read about it in the paper, I knew who it was and could go and find out what might be done, not as a "Christmas basket Christian" but as a friend—because we were already friends at the station.

But that first morning after I left Charlie I drove on to my office downtown and went into the indoor parking lot. The same thing happened. "Good morning, Mr. Miller." Only this time I was "easier" and found out that Al had a family too (all this in a few minutes without keeping him from his work). I was discovering that if one is really interested, he can soon find out a great deal about people—in a few minutes a day.

Men and women seemed to come out of the woodwork that day in the First National Building where my office was, people I had never really seen as *persons:* the old gentleman who ran the elevator, the secretaries in the office, the bank teller, the head-waiter at the Petroleum Club. Although I could not speak to them all that day, I found that just a question, an interested ear, and one might create a "thirty-second island" of caring in a person's otherwise impersonal day. In the months to come I saw these sketchy outlines develop into the foundations of some real relationships for Christ and for me.

For years I had been trying to witness to those I considered to be "important," and the people along my daily path might as well have been trees walking by me. It was as if I were opening my eyes for the first time and seeing the world of the present moment. I was finding a life-sized life at last—a life that wasn't so far beyond my ability that it left me continually frustrated, exhausted, or guilty.

I began to realize, emotionally as well as intellectually, that I was discovering a way to live out my days in the business world in a new relationship with God's people, a way that was making it possible for me to find reality in simple day-by-day contacts, since I now felt that these had significance for God.

I had thought before that I had to be a big churchman to do big things for God. Consequently, most of my "Christian work" was frustrating and left me miserable, because its success depended on my manipulating other people into my program. But as I looked around me and found the people and work in my own world to be real, I began to feel more and more the sense of being on a secret mission of faith for Christ. I was creatively trying to learn how to love people on their terms and to pray for them. Occasionally, there were some disappointments and rejections. Some people have forgotten how to respond to the personal in life, and I had to be careful not to get people in trouble who had to "run" to get their jobs done and had been told not to talk to people while working. My motives were occasionally misunderstood (and were bad sometimes). I don't know what my beginning to see *persons* did for the people I knew, but it certainly changed me. I had a sense of "having time" for people and the exciting feeling of being on "new ground," on which I was not just imitating the most outstanding Christians I knew.

The focus of life was almost imperceptibly changing from the distant horizon of tomorrow or next month to the immediate present, the *now*. I saw that so much of my life had been spent in a world of unreality. I was either regretting (or at least reliving) incidents and relationships in my past, or I was envisioning great conquests or possible tragedies in the future. Now I can see that the past is only a dream. I cannot affect it or change it. It is no longer changeable. And the future is equally unreal, since it does not yet even exist. As a matter of fact I realized that the only *real* time there is, or ever has been in which to live and act, is now—the present moment.* No decision, no birth, no death, nothing ever happened in a future or a past moment, only in a present one. And I had filled so many of the present moments of my life with the unreality of the past or future. The blinding introspection in which I had spent so much time had again and again blurred the intensity of my attention from seeing the *actual* opportunities and relationships that stood waiting before my eyes. I had marched into the future looking straight ahead—passing by the unconsciously searching eyes of those people beside the road which I was traveling.

This simple change of the focus of my attention to the immediate events of the moment as the important events—from God's perspective—made me realize that all of my background and training were not a kind of "practicing" preparing me for some big public Christian position sometime in the future. (I used to wonder, "What is all this hell training me for?") I now began to see that all my past was training me for the events and encounters of *this day*, however insignificant this day may seem from my perspective. Each day, each relationship, in my business life began to take on new importance. God might have something new to do in *this* relationship. I saw in the Scriptures that the days on which Christ was born, crucified, and rose from the dead did *not* seem important *as they were happening* even to most of the people present, but *only* to those who saw the events of those days from God's perspective. I began to realize that I could easily miss out on the things God may be doing in *this* day—the seeds he is planting, the new visions of renewal, the despair he wants to heal, the hope he wants to fulfill in a life—unless I began to

---

* I am indebted to Howard Butt for bringing this idea forcibly to my attention in a talk to a conference group at Laity Lodge.

see the possibilities of his healing action all around me along the pathways he will send me *this hour.*

In a way, this may sound easy, but it is *not.* The discipline of living in the now is the most difficult I know; I fail constantly, sometimes for weeks. But paradoxically, there is real power in this sort of living. The people who give themselves to the present moment are also giving themselves more wholly to the people they are with at that moment. If you and I are together, and I am unconsciously glancing at my watch, fretting about the next hour or appointment or later event, *you* are going to be less open than if you have my complete attention *right now.* You experience my lack of attention as a lack of interest in *you.* So, almost automatically by living in the present, every relationship is potentially more real, is potentially more life-changing. Also, if I think of *this* as the important moment in our relationship, I find that I am not quite as likely to manipulate you now or butter you up in order that you may do something for me in the future. For I am trying to hear and deal with the meanings of what you are saying and doing now. Whereas when my focus of attention is on future goals (however noble), my present words and actions toward you are almost always edited toward shaping your opinion or action for the accomplishment of my goal later.

Also, as I have listened and watched people who seem to be alive to the present situation in which they find themselves, I have discovered a profound experience of "life" or "presence" when I am with them. This is true whether the person is an actor on the Broadway stage or a teacher working with tough Christian businessmen. This sort of aliveness is winsome and makes me more alive as I respond to the Life I see in them. It draws me toward that Life. It is as if our attention were a powerful spotlight, the beam of which God lets us direct. We can shine this beam off into the past or future or into the eyes of the people around us in the present. When people focus their interest deeply into my life, something happens between us—we move into the warmer arena of the "personal"—the situation changes, and I am suddenly alive with them . . . I began to see that agape love rides down the beam of our attention into people's hearts. And I think that this basic attention to individuals in the present moment may be the greatest kind of love we can give them. For in a strange way we are giving them our lives in that instant, when we are giving them our whole attention. I have come to believe that this is perhaps the most real way to value persons as human beings—to really be *with* them and take them seriously as they are. A single such contact may change the whole direction of a life, a single experience of helping someone realize that he or she is really of some value.

Several years ago a girl came several hundred miles to a conference I was also attending at Laity Lodge. In a small group we were talking about the people who had had the greatest influence in our lives. The last person to speak was this very attractive young woman in her twenties. She told us that when she was about twelve years old, Elton Trueblood was speaking in the city in which she lived. He was staying in her parents' home. She told us that during the day or two he was there, he talked to her, asked her questions, and listened to what *she* had to say, just as he did to her parents. She said that although he never knew it, that brief experience as a young girl of being taken as an authentic, intelligent Christian had made her want deeply to be one, and had changed the direction of her life.

I guess what I am saying is that in trying to find a way to live a simple, natural life for Christ in the midst of the action of common living, I am finding that what I have always thought of as the *process*, the daily living, has become the *end*. It is as if God had adjusted the lenses of my eyes so that people and objects in the present, which had been blurred and indistinct as I stared toward the horizon, have taken on a new sharpness and reality. And because the present has become absorbing, I no longer feel the haunting need to get *further on* to some undefined something in my Christian life in the future. Some of us are learning to turn again and again to the Lord of the present moment to find the eternal quality of life of which Christ spoke (John 17:3).

Not long ago I heard a story that helped me see again the paradoxical power in living in the *now*. Several years ago a very busy business executive in an eastern city was rushing to catch a train. He had about given up trying to live a "personal" daily life because of the great demands on his time—speaking engagements and administrative duties in his organization. This particular morning en route to Grand Central Station he promised himself that he would try to *be* a Christian that day instead of only talking about it. By the time he had picked up his ticket, he was late. Charging across the lobby with his bags and down the ramp, he heard the last "all aboard." He was about to get on the train when he bumped into a small child with his suitcase. The little boy had been carrying a new jigsaw puzzle, the pieces of which were now scattered all over the platform.

The executive paused, saw the child in tears, and with an inward sigh, stopped, smiled, and helped the boy pick up his puzzle, as the train pulled out.

The child watched him intently. When they finished picking up all of the pieces, the little boy looked at the man with a kind of awe. "Mister," he said hesitantly, "are you *Jesus?*"

And for the moment the man realized that—on that platform, in that little boy's life—he had been.

With Regard to the Matter of "Christian Love"

For some years this question bothered me in the growing company of changing lives. There was more talk of "Christian love" than I was used to. Although I felt loved and accepted by many of these turned-on Christians in a way I never had before, I was uneasy about my own lack of selfless (agape) love for many of them. I did love some of them, but usually they were either the attractive ones or those who evidenced a real concern about me, and I knew that this was the same old "swapout," marketplace love Erich Fromm and others described so well as characteristic of our capitalistic and consumer type living.[1] Yet, although I did not *feel* very loving much of the time, I had to admit that in my daily living I was helping people I had not even noticed before. And I was doing things as a Christian to reach out to people in situations I had always ignored. This was taking place sort of naturally as I began to see people from the new perspective into which I was moving. But there was seldom the warm selfless feeling I had always thought should be central to the experience of Christian love. I prayed about this, read about it, and asked about it. Although some Christians confessed that they too did not really have much Christian love for the unlovely and it concerned them, this was little comfort to me.

One day as I was thinking about this question of the experience of Christian love, a scene flashed onto the screen of my imagination. I was sitting on our front porch and our youngest daughter was riding her tricycle down the driveway toward the street. I noticed that from up the block a huge moving van was coming very fast. The driver's brake had slipped, and he was moving faster and faster down the hill in front of our house. In a horrified moment I realized that my little girl was heading out into the street right in front of that truck, and that because of a hedge she could not see the truck coming! Without even thinking, I jumped across the porch rail and ran for the street, realizing at the last second that I could dive and push the tricycle beyond the wheels, but that I could never make it out of the way myself. Then I was diving. Just as I pushed the tricycle beyond the truck, I felt and heard a horrible *crunch* as the huge wheel ran right across my back. . . . Even though this scene took place only in my imagination, I was weak just thinking about it. Here was a real act of love, "laying down one's life," and I hoped I would do that if the situation ever actually came up.

But as I sat there thinking about this, a nasty little kid from down the street came riding by in front of our house. He's the one who picks his nose all the time and who had laughed and made nasty signs at me when I had tried to catch him to talk to him about throwing rocks at my little girl the day before. Although I like most kids, I do not like this one. But as I watched him ride by, the same scene I had been through a few minutes before started replaying itself in my imagination. Only this time the nasty little boy was the one riding down our driveway toward the path of the hurtling truck. I hesitated; this wasn't my child. But then, although I did not even *like* the boy, I found myself jumping the rail and running for the street. Again I dove and pushed the tricycle beyond the truck's wheels. And again I was crushed.

In thinking about these two experiences, the haunting question came to my mind: *Which of these two was the greater act of Christian love? To save your own daughter or the kid from down the street?* And the answer I could not shake was *to die for the child down the street.* Any pagan would try to save his own daughter. And yet there was *no warm feeling of love at all* in the second loving act. I had not even *wanted* to help him. Now I began to get excited. If this were true, then perhaps Christian love is not what I had always thought it was. I went back to the New Testament to see what love looked like there in light of this new experience.

Turning first to the thirteenth chapter of First Corinthians, I saw that love is the most important gift and will outlast all the others. To examine Christian love in action, I thought: *Where* *would I turn to see the greatest example of God's kind of love in action?* And, of course, I thought of Christ's giving of himself. As I read the accounts of Christ's life, I saw something I had never seen before. I was rereading the gospel reports of the last hours before the Crucifixion. Here was the One who had come to Jerusalem, no doubt with an awareness of the personal danger this trip involved. He had looked at Jerusalem and wept. Now he was coming toward some sort of climax in his sense of mission. Then there is that strange scene in Gethsemane (Matthew 26; Luke 22). Jesus leaves even his most trusted friends and goes off a little way by himself to pray about continuing in the direction his life and ministry seemed to be taking. As I read, I thought: *Now here is real love in action. Here Jesus is approaching the act that changed the world's conception of what love in human form is like. Why can't I feel that way about loving people?* But as I read on I was shocked. I read the account again. What I thought I had seen was true. Jesus was evidently not filled with a warm feeling of loving desire to die for people. As a matter of fact, our term for extreme discomfort, "sweating blood," likely came from his experience that night. He evidently "sweated blood" and prayed three times for a way not to have to perform this most loving act. And when he did agree to go, the love was expressed not by his *feeling* but by the fact that he acted out of obedience and love for his Father *whether he felt like it or not!**

---

* I am aware of the controversy over the source of several of these verses and that my use of this scene bypasses the whole question of what Jesus in his humanity actually knew in the garden about the ultimate value of the next day's actions. But my point is that whatever he knew he apparently based his decision in facing the crisis of risking his life not on a warm feeling about the results of the action nor its benefits to others but on his loving obedience to his Father's will as he could determine it. For a brief but excellent scholarly treatment of the human-divine question regarding Jesus see *The Humanity and Divinity of Christ* by John Knox, Cambridge University Press, 1967.

Wow! If this is true, then Christian love is not based on the feeling I had always longed for. Christian love is simply an act of the kind God wants performed for another person's health and wholeness to help fulfill God's will for that person. And my *performing* that act in Christ's perspective and concern is the *love*, not my warm feeling *about* doing it. Then I began to see that all through the Scriptures and the church's history the greatest acts of love were often accompanied by circumstances that must have been very unpleasant and distasteful for the Christian. I realized that I had always interpreted the joyful obedience to God which these acts demonstrated as a "warm feeling" *about the unpleasant act*. Evidently, I had assumed that Paul's beatings and the fires of martyrdom or the nails of the Cross didn't really hurt because of the warm Hollywood-type feeling of love. Further, I had noticed before that Christ *commanded* his disciples to love one another (John 13:34, 35). I saw why that command had disturbed me in the past. *No one* can command *his feelings* for others. But one *can* command to a far greater degree his concerned *actions* toward others.

So now I realized that from Christ's perspective I was not to pray for a feeling of love for my fellow human beings, but rather for the courage to act in love toward them in specific situations, whatever my spiritual temperature read at the time, or whether or not I felt loving that day. And the strangest thing began to happen. Occasionally the feeling I had longed for about people has come along after the act of love or concern has passed or in the midst of it. It then became clear that this feeling is a gift that may or may not accompany the act of love.

But there is a problem here. If one is loving others out of "obedience," people have told me, the "good turns" are cold and impersonal and cause resentment on the part of the party being loved. But I am not talking about *that* kind of attitude. The kind of specific love I am referring to is paradoxical. *Because* of Christ, I will find myself doing the loving act *for* the person. In other words, from the recipient's perspective you are not acting toward him impersonally, out of duty to a remote God, but the person *feels loved* as you move toward him into his life space. This paradoxical truth keeps this kind of love from being a legalistic obligation . . . which would certainly be recognized as such by the recipient.

In any case, I have quit beating myself with a chain when I do not feel love. I am free to begin finding natural ways to bring the kind of love and concern to people which I would want to bring if I felt the warm feeling.* I believe now that my greatest days of loving from Christ's perspective may be those days on which I don't even feel well, much less loving. And yet I reach out toward another person in his perhaps hostile franticness, simply because this is Christ's way and I feel that he would want me to do the simple act with which I am confronted. And, of course, there is emotional feeling involved in such acts, but not the kind I had looked for.

---

* It is interesting to note that many psychologists following Guthrie *et al.* have long believed that contrary to common belief, feelings follow behavior change instead of preceding it. (For instance, an alcoholic, perhaps out of sheer desperation, forces himself to go to an AA meeting, not feeling like it at all. But once he has taken the step and changed his behavior to the extent of going, he may come to have feelings of hope for a new life—instead of a wonderful, hopeful feeling coming first, convincing him to quit drinking.) Whereas, for years we Christians have tried to get our attitudes right first, I am saying that my experience has been that if I begin acting in love, often the feeling of love will follow.

MEMORANDUM

TO: Bruce

FROM: Keith

RE: Chapter 5, Relationship Pressures and Changes Because of Contact With God

My material about "living in the now" and "Christian love" seems awfully long-winded as I read it over. (But as you know this is not exactly a brand-new problem with me.)

If we are going to talk about close-in relationship changes and pressures that result from commitments, we've got to mention something about the relationships in our homes and with those hard to cope with people we smash into emotionally in our everyday living—a "relational" approach to loving. Again I guess I am asking for some specific kinds of directional guidelines that you've found helpful.

K.

❖ SOME YEARS AGO, IN THE MIDDLE OF A comfortable luncheon meeting of Christian businessmen in midtown Manhattan, a Congregational minister from New England, Lee Whiston, dropped a bomb when he asked us, "Are you fun to live with?"

Most of the regular members of the group had from time to time confessed problems pertaining to their families. But with Lee's question, our traditional Christian concern for our families was shattered. Lee suggested that if we were living as Christ would have us, our families would enjoy living with us.

Well, we have never forgotten Lee's question, and each of us began to live with it daily and later referred to it in the group from time to time. God used that question to check my own motives and attitudes. Why do I want my wife or my children "to be more Christian" at times? Is it because I want God's best for them or because I want God to change some annoying trait in their lives that is creating a problem in mine? Is my motive really love—or am I using God to nag my family?

Several years ago when I had been having a faithful devotional time each morning (and my wife had not), I greeted her very irritably at the breakfast table. She had the Christian love to suggest that if this was all my "quiet time" was producing, maybe it would be better for me to spend the time in bed. Going to work on the bus that morning, I saw how I had been misusing that time in the morning, and was only feeding my self-righteousness. If I had really been spending time in God's presence, it would have made me a different person at the breakfast table.

The home is the most difficult—and rewarding—place for any Christian to put his faith to work. It's much easier to be effective and loving and faithful and gentle with people we see only from time to time. Unfortunately, we cannot fool the people who share our home. I am convinced that *we are what we are at home!*

Years ago I actually thought my family held me back spiritually.

Now I see that God has given me at least one place where I can test how far I have come in this new life and relationship he offers.

The home is the place where Christ can speak most clearly. I would rather hear God speak through almost anyone else than through my wife or my children. I can "take it" when he speaks through the minister, or through a friend, or through a book, or through his Word. But to recognize God speaking through my wife's loving rebuke or suggestion takes a great deal more grace. And if God is to speak clearly, whom can he better use than the one who sees me most clearly, loves me most unreservedly, and understands my needs most deeply?

At the heart of our Christian conviction is the belief that God wills newness of life, peace, joy, and love, not only for individuals, but for families. Here are four things we feel God has been trying to show our family over the years, so that we can cooperate with his purpose and plan for us.

The first is the most difficult. *If you really want God to make your home new, you must let him begin with you.* It is difficult for the member of the family, whether parent or child, who thinks he is "furthest along spiritually" to make the first move in a total surrender of his will and life to Christ. The instinctive thing is to hope that the others will catch up to us, so that we can "go all the way" together. This is never the case. One member of the family must be the spiritual pioneer and become vulnerable to the others to initiate God's action in a home.

I remember a couple who were married for nine years and who were living in hell. She claimed that he was romantically and emotionally cold and escaped from the home at every opportunity. She was involved in many civic and social and church organizations to find meaning for her life. Her husband, on the other hand, detested the kind of homemaking and cooking that his wife did (or rather did not do) and said that he could not feel warm toward someone who was so irresponsible in the home. Each declared that should the other change, he or she would follow suit.

One day the wife came to see me, on the verge of a divorce. I will never forget the miracle that began to happen when she promised God, on her knees, that she would be everything that her husband wanted her to be as a homemaker. She went home then, not out of a sense of duty but out of a new and deeper experience of God's love, and began to minister to her husband out of the fullness of that love. It took about a year for the husband to respond totally and to face up to the person God wanted to make of him as a husband.

Many of us live in a stalemate and cry, "Unfair! Unfair!" But the only way to break the stalemate is for one to go all the way. Each going halfway is never God's solution for a marriage. *

There is an amazing verse in 1 Peter 3:1 that says, "You wives, be submissive to your husbands, so that some, though they do not obey the word, may be won without a word by the behavior of their wives." (That verse applies equally to husbands!) How wise the Apostle Peter was in sensing that we are not to talk about our faith at home, or if we do, to talk very sparingly. The thing that counts is to live a new and radiant life day by day and to be "fun to live with."

A second thing that our family must learn again and again is *how to love in God's way*. We are all aware of how children learn to manipulate their parents. They know how to "butter up" father for an increase in allowance, the use of the car, or permission to do something usually forbidden. Unfortunately, most adults relate to each other in just the same way only with more sophistication.

When God's love captures us and we have the resources from

---

* In cases where one's partner is an addict or an alcoholic, it is very helpful for the partner deciding to be vulnerable to seek counseling and/or help from Al-Anon or another Twelve Step group.

within to live out the pattern for love described by the Apostle Paul in 1 Corinthians 13, we no longer have to manipulate people, but are free to be vulnerable to them and to their demands. This is what Christ meant in the great commandment to love one another as he has loved us. We have the promise that this kind of love never fails.

God's love working through us is permissive and unconditional. That means it is not conditioned by the response we get from people but by God's abundant supply in us. It offers freedom to others rather than rigidity. It is unproductive to force family prayers or church attendance on an unwilling spouse or grown children. If Jesus Christ has truly made us new, we then have the resources to live so that they may *want* to pray and worship with us.

My wife and I laugh often at how we must continually learn to give love in terms meaningful to the other. Each of us would rather give love in the ways that we enjoy giving rather than in the ways the other enjoys receiving. How many hundreds of times in our many years of marriage have I come home to a freshly baked pie. When God has spoken to her and convicted her of some failure in our relationship, she has often expressed her love or repentance by baking a pie. Now I don't especially like pie, but I have had to eat an awful lot of it.

In the same way, I have come home ready to hug and kiss and whisper sweet nothings to a spouse with whom I was most unloving or in violent disagreement a few hours earlier. At such times romance is the last thing that she wants from me!

We keep learning from God what to do after he has changed one of our hearts. We need to ask him *how* to express this new love that we feel, so that the other can receive it unmistakably. God wants to love people through us and he has to show us his unique strategy for loving each person he sends us.

One of my favorite contemporary theological works is the

comic strip "Peanuts." Some time ago poor old Charlie Brown was coming home from a baseball game muttering, "One hundred and forty to nothing! . . . I just don't understand it! . . . And we were *so sincere!*" How often I have been sincere in expressing a new love God has given me for someone at home or in the office or elsewhere, but my strategy was all wrong. We need more than sincerity and a change of heart. We need to let the Holy Spirit show us how he can get through us in ways that will be meaningful to those on the receiving end.

I received a great deal of help a few years ago from a small group we belonged to in Illinois. One couple was concerned about a pre-school daughter, their only child. The father, who was extremely busy in all manner of church, civic, and scouting activities, felt that he was so out of touch with his daughter that he would have to drop some worthwhile activities and spend more time with her. He tried this with no result. One night he came to the group ex-cited. He told us that God had revealed to him that it was not more time that his daughter needed but *all of him* for a brief time each day. He had been aware that when he was playing games with her or reading to her or doing anything with her he always had part of his mind on something else, or was carrying on a conversation with his wife, or was watching TV. His daughter never had more than half of him. She reacted to this (as all of us do) and had all the symptoms of being unloved and rejected.

When God showed this man that one of the ways to love is to give another one's undivided attention, the relationship with his daughter took on a new dimension. This same thing is true for husbands and wives, brothers and sisters, roommates, and all others with whom we are in contact.

The third lesson our family is learning has to do with *total honesty*. Real communication between God and people or between human beings requires a serious attempt at total honesty.

Most of us hide behind our masks and pretend to be people we are not. How hungry our family is to know us as we really are and to be known as they really are.

Our children need to know of our past failures and of the mistakes we made when we were their age. They also need to know of our present failures and where we need forgiveness today. If in our family prayers we can be honest about ourselves, we do more to introduce our children to God than in all of our prayers for them. As a matter of fact, we must do much more praying with them. (It is best to pray *for* them in our private devotions.) In marriage we need to open our hearts totally to a spouse and learn to say, "I am sorry," or, "I was wrong" at the appropriate times.

What happens when our children see us lose our tempers or behave unfairly or unjustly and then in family prayers pray for all the missionaries around the world and the minister in the church and Aunt Martha and Uncle Jim? They know this is phony and is not really being honest with God at all. When we can include prayers for our present needs (of which they are all too aware), they will almost invariably respond to the reality of Christ themselves.

The main thing to remember, it seems to me, is this: never hesitate to be honest about your own faults, but always hesitate being honest about someone else's.

I believe that God will show us how to say things to others about their needs in those rare times that require it. One Christmas morning I received a handsomely wrapped package from my youngest son, which turned out to be a bottle of deodorant. On the card were the words, "Not because you do. So that you won't!" What tact! I have often wished that when it did seem right to talk to someone else in the family about his needs, I could have the gift to say things that discreetly.

As we meet in prayer and discussion groups, we need to be honest about some of the desperate situations we get into as families. I remember sitting at lunch with a group in Ontario who were talking about marriage. One of the women, a charming person of early middle years, was telling about her own past and present difficulties with a problem husband (the only kind God makes!). Someone asked, "Did you ever think of divorce?" She replied with a perfectly blank face, "Divorce? No! Murder? Yes!"

We all laughed and from that point the conversation took an entirely different turn. We began to be honest about the cost of being God's people as husbands and wives together. That kind of honesty in any Christian group is a gift.

The final thing that I personally struggle most with is *letting others in the family minister to me*. As a clergyman, I have an idea that I must always be right and the source of all Christian truth. Christ tries to show me that he is in my home independently of me and that some of his greatest truths come not only from my wife but from my children, even the youngest. God is there and he is working and I must enjoy being on the receiving end as others are used by Christ to minister to me. I believe that I am becoming free of having to bring Christ to my family. I might add that it is a great deal more fun to discover him already here in our midst.

However, the battle is not easy. About a year ago I was having a difficult relationship with a wonderful Christian man. He seemed to judge me and criticize me no matter what I did. One day he wrote me a letter that made me furious, and I brought it home to my wife. "How in the world can I answer this?" I grumbled and showed it to her. She made several suggestions that I disposed of quickly because I didn't think she understood the devious nature of this man's spirit.

Finally she turned to me and said, "Why don't you take the advice you're so free to give all the rest of us?" (I knew something was coming!)

"What is that?" I asked.

"Why don't you admit to God that you have no love in your heart for this man and ask him to change you?"

"That's ridiculous!" I shouted, and stomped out of the room to read the evening paper until dinner was ready.

That night in saying prayers with my daughter, I had to face what I knew God had been trying to say to me through my wife. I asked his forgiveness in my daughter's presence and asked God to change me. My daughter concluded her prayers by saying, "Lord, you know that Father is a difficult man to change, and yet we know you can do it, and I ask you to give him your love for this man."

Now this is not the role I would have chosen for myself. I would rather be the teacher, the prophet, and the authority in my home. But frankly, that does not always work, and lately I've begun to enjoy being a learner with my family at the feet of Jesus Christ.

Coping With the Unlovely Stranger

If there is a strategy of love that we can begin to apply at home, that same approach ought to work with the people we meet every day, friends or strangers. But it isn't easy.

At five o'clock on a winter Wednesday I entered New York's Port Authority bus terminal. I was hurrying home for a quick dinner and then on to conduct a midweek service at a nearby church. The usual crowd was lined up behind the escalators that take suburban passengers to their buses. Briefcase in one hand and newspaper in the other, I got in line and began the commuter shuffle.

Just as I got to the head of the line, a grim-faced woman came up from the side, shoved in front of me, planted her elbow in my stomach, and stepped onto the escalator.

Now I maintain that there is nothing easy about the Christian life, and every year I see more clearly the complications of radical obedience to Christ. What should I say to such a person? I know what I would have said a few years ago—but I am no longer free to put someone like that "in her place." I know what I would *like* to say. I would like to be a Saint Francis kind of Christian who genuinely loves birds and flowers and children and even rude and thoughtless women—but I haven't arrived at that stage yet.

Being somewhere in between my former condition and my ideal one, I removed the woman's elbow from my stomach and said with elaborate sarcasm, "Forgive me. I didn't mean to shove you."

Her reaction was devastating. She turned, and since she was only a step or two ahead, she looked me straight in the eye. Her face seemed to fall apart. "I don't understand it," she said with apology and shock. "Why are you so nice to me? I was really rude—I shouldn't have shoved in line like that."

I was at a loss for words. The woman had reacted to my counterfeit display of love as if it were real, and for the moment, at least, she was transformed. It is quite possible that the woman had been fighting all her life for a place in line. Perhaps she had been raised in a big family where she had to contend for favors and affection. Even now in some office she might be fighting for promotions or benefits or a preferred place on the vacation list. Perhaps this was the first time that someone with whom she was fighting for a place in line had stepped back and given in to her.

At this point I was ashamed of the pettiness of my reaction, but I gathered my wits enough to mumble something like, "It doesn't hurt to be nice to people." Then I ran headlong for my bus.

Headed for New Jersey, I sat in bewildered embarrassment. "Lord," I prayed silently, "how can I preach tonight? What are you trying to teach me?"

Finally he seemed to say, "Bruce, I have been trying to tell you, and all my people for centuries, that life upon this earth will not be changed by preaching and teaching and committees, but by people giving up their rightful place in line—every kind of line—simply because I gave up my rightful place when I came to earth to be among you. What I ask is that you who profess to believe in me do the same. My strategy of love will always release a chain reaction of changed lives."

I never step onto the escalator now without looking about wistfully for someone to slam in ahead of me—but no one does! How radically different is what Jesus has in mind for me: He wants me to give up my rightful place in my home, office, professional circle, church, neighborhood. If I am not alert to those who are fighting for first place, my instinct will be to hang on to what is mine and put the offender in his place. But if I can remember my Lord's strategy and with his help give up what is rightfully mine, I may see miracles.

A Strategy of Love

This approach to love, that God can give us, involves some very basic ingredients that can apply to any relationship. First of all, people respond more to how we feel about them than to what we say to them.

I have a friend who is extremely self-conscious. When he comes into a room where there are small children, he tries to ignore them, hiding behind a newspaper or book, or becoming absorbed in television. But invariably the children, whether they are his relatives or total strangers, climb all over him and refuse to leave him alone, even though he says, "Go away and stop bothering me." Children are not put off by his gruff exterior. They know that it hides a warm and genuine love.

On the other hand, these same children will sometimes run from a sweet old relative who says, "Come here, dear, and give

Auntie a big kiss." They sense that actually she is no lover of little children.

For years Dr. John Casteel said to students at Union Theological Seminary in New York that dynamic Christian truth is transmitted *relationally* rather than *propositionally*, though he conceded that it is often a difficult truth for seminary students to comprehend, since their focus is so much on the theological content of the Bible.

I often ask people about the person who most influenced their lives and what that person did. A frequent answer is: "The person who most influenced me in my life treated me as an equal." The person was in some superior role, either because of age or experience or status. Nevertheless, he did not use that superior position as a platform from which to help but was able to stand alongside the other person. Remember how Jesus washed the feet of the disciples and told us to do the same! D. T. Niles, of Ceylon, said that the Christian church often misses the mark because we Christians would rather *give a service than be a servant.* The servant identifies with the person he is serving and is willing to be a subordinate. There is a vast difference between this and bringing another a service he needs, whether it be food, medicine, teaching, or counseling!

A few months ago a woman told several of us about a prayer and study group she had organized in her suburban neighborhood. For months this lovely woman had tried to help the "lost" in her neighborhood, but with little success. The group seemed hopeless. One morning she had a rare fight with her husband and the group was to meet that afternoon. At first she thought she would have to stay away. When she finally went, she broke down and told of what had happened, and concluded by saying, "I have no right to teach you. I shouldn't even be here in this condition!" Then guilt overwhelmed her and she left hurriedly. She was afraid that she had completely lost her effectiveness, only to find later that three of the young housewives made tremendous spiritual advances that day because their teacher had demonstrated that she was "one of them." If she was really like them *in their needs*, they concluded, they wanted to know her Lord!

Listening. "He was always interested in hearing about my problems and my ideas" is another description of influential friends. We mistakenly think that our knowledge or insight is the greatest gift we can give to others. Often we bring them much further when we eagerly listen to what they are trying to say about themselves and their problems. We affirm their worth and dignity by taking them seriously.

It is illuminating to study Jesus' way with individuals. He often got a "case history." Jesus would draw out the demon-possessed, or those sick or in trouble, by asking the person what he understood of his own problem. The Holy Spirit may do more to convict a person out of his own mouth by what he says to a loving listener than by all of the good advice and insight that may come from the mouth of another.

Personal Honesty. "He let me know what his own problems and needs were" is another description I often hear concerning people who have influenced others. One hears a great deal of concern expressed that religion can become "too personal." But Jesus must have practiced this kind of honesty. For example, the only way we could know about his temptations in the wilderness is that he must have told his disciples, for no one else was there.

Paul Tournier, the eminent Swiss physician, has contributed much to the field of counseling and psychotherapy along this line. Dr. Tournier is successful because he is honest about himself with his patients and does not relate merely as a professional person to a client. He relates as a person to a person. It is amazing how God uses this to build therapeutic relationships.

One evening as a men's group was meeting in our office in New York, a man came in whom no one knew. Each thought that he had been referred by someone else in the circle, and so it was suggested he pull up a chair and join the six or eight men who were meeting for fellowship and prayer. He sat and listened as several individuals talked about present struggles toward becoming whole people and effective Christians.

Finally the leader turned to the stranger and asked who he was. "My name is Paul," he said, "and as long as you have been honest, I will be honest too. I am a dope addict. I came here to rob this office to get a fix, but I think I have found something better." Paul stayed to pray and asked God for help with his serious problem simply because he heard some other men being honest.

Vulnerability. "He trusted me." That is another quality characteristic of those who have shaped people's lives. We need to trust others in costly ways even as Jesus trusted Judas, not only with his money but with his reputation and his life. It seems to me that this is one of Jesus' supreme messages for us, and in John 13:34 he commands us to love one another as he has loved us.

To be vulnerable to one another is hardly possible apart from the presence of God. How afraid we are that the other will take advantage of us if we don't moralize and preach to him about his problems. I recently had an effective Christian tell me that one of the secrets of his life is, "Never let another person's sins bother you until they bother him." If we really live this out, we will become involved with people in a costly way.

Willingness to Receive. "This person would often ask me to help him or pray for him" is another description of a life-shaper. Jesus frequently initiated a new relationship by asking for help. He was never reluctant to ask for food or lodging or water or even company in his loneliness and temptation. This was Jesus' first step in graciously opening other lives for the help they needed from him. We need to discover how to receive help from others so that they may then accept what God may want to give them through us. As one friend of mine often says, "Don't be a stingy receiver."

Several years ago, I became suddenly ill at a conference in Bloomington, Illinois. I had all the usual symptoms that go with the flu, including chills and fever. I took to my bed in the men's dormitory. Within the space of one hour, six different people heard about my need and came to offer help. One anointed me with oil for healing—my first experience of this ancient rite of the church. Another knelt and offered prayer. The third person was a woman doctor who dosed me with aspirin, took my pulse, and reassured me that, in all probability, I had a twenty-four-hour flu bug. The fourth person brought me a tray of food, the last thing in the world I wanted at that time! The fifth just expressed concern, while the sixth, a wonderful Finnish masseuse, came in and sang hymns in her native language while she gave me a massage.

Two things happened. First, I was healed within the hour. I don't know which one of those people was the channel of God's healing, but I suspect they all were used. But second, and even more exciting, I became aware that God was trying to teach me how important it is to receive help from him through others. It is much easier for me to give than to receive, which has often been a block in relationships. I still thank God for that lesson and am grateful for my six "teachers."

So God communicates his life through us to others. The apostolic succession of new life from person to person is a twentieth-century reality unbroken since Pentecost.

As we begin to relate to people in at least these five ways with identification, listening, honesty, vulnerability, and a willingness to receive, we are practicing a strategy of love that communicates.

CHAPTER SIX

❖

THE FAMILY

MEMORANDUM

TO: Keith

FROM: Bruce

RE: Chapter 6, The Family

Maybe it's a good thing we got together on this project. Your mind and mine are amazingly complementary. I had to smile last week as we talked on the phone when you said, "When I get panicky and think I'm boring people or am in over my head, I always start talking in dramatic stories." Well, when *I'm* unsure or feel that things are getting beyond me, I start *making lists*. And as I look back over the book so far, it's mostly stories and lists. Maybe *no one* knows how to talk about the kinds of things that happen in a person's private thoughts when he tries to commit his life to Christ. In a way that's comforting. It leaves us free to try since there are no "experts" when it comes to loving God and allowing ourselves to be loved.

Although I wrote some things about the family earlier, I think we should do some more in this area. Hazel and I have been involved in lots of conferences, churches, and theological discussions, but the sticky wickets still keep coming up as we try to grow in our family life. Why don't you tell something about the paradox of being relatively free and yet still facing the power-insecurity struggle that goes on behind the scenes in marriage. I think one reason we preachers tend to get abstract about our communication is in order to avoid the pain of facing our fears and failures at home. (If this request makes you nervous, just report it in "story" form.)

B.

❖ M<small>Y FIRST ACT AFTER DRIVING HOME</small> from my initial serious commitment encounter with God was to pour myself a tall scotch and water and think it over. Something had happened to me inside which both frightened and excited me. It was as if my swollen soul had been lanced and the poison drawn out; and I was clean. I had a new chance at life in a way I did not understand but felt deeply to be true. I didn't dare tell my wife for fear she would think I had snapped mentally. When this thought occurred to me I burned my journal describing the hell of the previous months, because I was afraid I *might* be mentally in trouble and this information might be used to have me committed someday. For the first time since I was a child I had a perspective of hope and challenge and completeness . . . a sense of direction.

At that time I remembered when I was a small boy waking up early on spring mornings and smelling the freshness of the earth and dreaming about those things life might have in store . . . even that day. Then, as I had grown up, I had "put away childish things" and had learned that life was hard and one did not live in continual expectancy. But now, as a grown man with a family, I began waking up and smelling the earth again. I kept waiting for this expectancy to go away, but it never has. Life became animated and real . . . although it began to happen in a way I would never have expected—given my religious preconceptions of what an honestly committed Christian life might be like.

The first inner change I can remember in those beginning months was that I started perceiving things I had never seen before in my own life and in the lives of everyone around me. It was almost as if God had issued me a new set of spiritual eyes. I was both horrified and fascinated by what I saw. For instance, from the time I can remember I had always been trained to be a humble, thoughtful, but hard-driving person. I had been kind to people and consciously felt very unworthy of all the little honors and attentions I had received along the way. But later, when I had been married a few months, I noticed that my wife did not see me as the unselfish person other people intimated I was. In fact she seemed to sense a great deal of *raw selfishness* in my makeup. I was, of course, keenly disappointed—because it was rather obvious to me that Mary Allen (though sweet and loving) was a spoiled and self-centered little girl!

But now suddenly as I looked at my life from this new perspective I saw that all my goodness and thoughtfulness to people—though consciously sincere for the most part—was a part of my overall life's mission . . . to build an unequaled reputation as a fine, successful, Christian-type man. Unconsciously I had needed to be right so much that I had paid an amazing price in terms of personal time spent being thoughtful to people. What I now saw which horrified me was that the only thing wrong with my life's plan was that it was (contrary to all my conscious beliefs) *totally self-centered*. It was totally calculated to bring honor to myself . . . though directed toward helping others. I realized with amazement that I am almost a complete egoist.

The next startling discovery I made was that I was basically a coward. This was a real blow; and my mind quickly marshaled dozens of acts and situations that belied this terrible revelation. But I knew it was true, though I had not consciously known before.

With these newly seen facts about myself came the realization that this combination (egoism and cowardice) is not only not uncommon even among Christians in our generation, but is in fact almost a formula for "success" in this country. From the time I was a small boy playing football I can remember tackling boys much larger than myself with great viciousness. My ego was so great that the opinion of the men and boys watching actually meant more to me than my physical well-being. I hit hard, not because I was tough—but in order to make sure no one would know that down inside I might not want to hit them at all.

In college I didn't stay up all night studying for final examinations because I had an insatiable hunger for a knowledge of economics. I stayed up all night to make sure that *I did not fail*. This combination forces a person to pay the price, whatever it is, for outward success and acclaim . . . but it doesn't make for much of a life inside, behind the mask where we really live. I found I was always "putting out fires" which might shed light on my true insecurity. But these basic faults in my makeup, even though I had not consciously faced them before, had actually worked to my apparent benefit all my life . . . that is, until I got married.

As I have stated, my young wife spotted at least my egoism right away. (It is not difficult to realize whether one's mate's attention is really focused on his or your interests.) I had hidden this self-centeredness so carefully from myself that I would fly into a frustrated and righteous rage when she would come close to revealing it to me. But after five years of marriage God was letting me see my own life and our marriage in a totally new light. I began to realize that I had never truly known what Christian marriage is. Oh, I could have said some doctrinally correct things about Christian marriage . . . a good many. But I couldn't seem to live them out at our address on a day in, day out basis. Now I began to discover existentially some strange things about marriage.

To begin with I saw that in marriage there is shared by the partners something analogous to that inmost secret consciousness in one's own deeply personal experience (which I have called the soul). There is an inner life in a marriage—a life that is lived out when two marriage partners are together with no one else present. This private arena can be more carefully recognized than you might think. There is a specific tone of voice people use. Sometimes a huge, booming, business tycoon's voice may take on a whining nasal quality in the intimate encounter with his wife in the soul of their marriage. The pillar of the "women of the church" who is all sweetness and light to the outer world may turn into a hissing, caustic hussy in the private arena of her marriage. There is a definite and highly communicative language marriage partners share at this level in their relationship—much of it unspoken. Each partner has a whole repertoire of "glances." A woman has her "angry" look; a man has his "I hate your guts" look. Or there is the "you're drinking too much, George," look. I have seen a woman nail her husband with a silent glance thirty feet across a crowded cocktail party . . . and watched him wilt as they shared the message intimately in the soul of their marriage . . . surrounded by a hundred oblivious people. The soul of a marriage can be a trysting place where two people can come together quietly from the struggles of the world and feel safe, accepted, and loved . . . or it can be a battleground where two egos are locked in a lifelong struggle for supremacy, a battle that is for the most part invisible to the rest of the world.

Another thing about this area of married life is that we soon place some articles of "furniture" in the soul of a marriage: some resentments, some jealousy, some situations that can be counted on unfailingly to bring anguish. These things begin to clutter up the soul of a marriage almost from the first night.

With this picture of the inner marriage life in mind, the basic practical problem of a marriage now seems to me to be this: two fine, healthy people wake up one morning and find themselves alone together in the soul of their marriage . . . realizing that they really don't know each other at all. What has happened is that each partner has come into marriage with his or her own vision of what a marriage ought to be.

A woman's vision of a husband depends on many things— what her father was like (and whether she idolized him or despised him), what novels she has read, what movies she has seen. All of her impressions of the ideal man for her, unconsciously for the most part, go into a composite image which she dreams her marriage partner will fulfill. A man's vision of a wife evolves in a similar fashion. In retrospect I think Mary Allen's vision was a balanced blend of a macho western cowboy, a smooth-talking and debonair talk-show host, and a cultured clergyman. And in all honesty, I think my premarital vision of an ideal wife was probably a combination of a Mother Teresa, a gorgeous soap opera leading lady, and television's most glib hostess and connoisseur of food and drink. But, of course, a wife not only has a vision of what a husband should be like, she also has a vision of what a *wife* should be. Any similarity between the husband's vision of an ideal wife and the wife's vision of an ideal wife is a rare and beautiful coincidence.

These different visions of the roles of each partner in a marriage constitute a good bit of the material for the frustrating struggles in the soul of the marriage. Many times the bride-to-be may have seen some basic difference in her vision of a husband and the actual man she is about to marry. But the aura of romance makes her feel that she can change the actual man to fit the mental image, thus making her total acceptance of him *conditional* . . . a fact which though unconscious to her becomes apparent to the husband quickly in a marriage's soul. Besides this, the young man may have been counting on the wife's changing to his vision. So what do we have?—two creators, *two gods*, in the soul of one marriage . . . each vying, each insisting on the validity of his or her own created image of what a husband and wife, what a marriage ought to be.

So the invisible battle lines are drawn across the soul of a marriage and the siege begins. This is not to say that there is not a great deal of happiness (physical and otherwise) in such a marriage. But in its soul there is at best a peaceful coexistence between two wills, a sort of stalemate with little pockets of resentment and hurt.

This is, I am convinced, an X-ray picture of many marriages within the leadership groups of Protestant churches in every city. And although the first five years of our marriage were, I had thought, the happiest of any couple I knew, the above description in many respects was a picture of our marriage from my perspective. For five years our relationship had been a good one with a lot of happiness and love and with a reasonably workable truce in its soul with regard to the battle of the wills. But our visions of marriage differed in several important respects.

The following example is almost unbelievable in showing how far we have come from the male chauvinism of 1949. But this was one way things were in many homes. My wife had been raised in a family with five daughters and no sons. Her father was of the old sexist southern school and didn't believe in men helping around the house with dishes, etc. But he made one concession in that he would take the trash basket in the kitchen out and empty it each evening for Mary Allen's mother. I had been raised with one brother. My father was also of the old southern male chauvinist background and he did not believe in helping with little household chores either . . . *especially* things like emptying the *trash basket*. When we got married and came home from our honeymoon, Mary Allen announced happily, "Honey, unlike some of my friends I don't want you to dry the dishes and mop the floors or make beds. These things are women's work." I was about to pop with thanksgiving, when she continued, "But I would appreciate it if you would take the trash basket in the kitchen out and empty it in the evenings."

I was stunned. I realized this was a very crucial point affecting my vision of a man and a husband.

"Honey, I'm sorry," I said slowly, "but I'm *not* taking out that wastebasket."

Now *she* was stunned . . . and a little angry.

"That's *all* I'm asking you to do!" she said in amazement.

"Honey, I'll work at night and *hire* someone to help you," I said determinedly, "but I'm not taking out that wastebasket." So the wastebasket in the kitchen became the first article of furniture in the soul of our marriage, which had to be stepped around almost daily in our relationship.

Another thing that characterized our marriage relationship was the overwhelming percentage of the instances in which I was deeply convinced that I was right, when we had arguments. I always had a justification for everything I did. Oh, I had given in all right—for strategic reasons—but I had felt very big about doing so.

With all of these little things, however, we had a fine marriage. I suppose (in retrospect) we were just trying to take the rough edges off each other in the soul of our marriage . . . with sandpaper. But then, five years later, I had gotten to the end of my mental rope that day beside the road in East Texas.

Then as I began to see the enormity of my ego and the subtlety of my selfishness, I soon had to bring this new perspective and knowledge into the soul of our marriage.

It happened like this: we were arguing about something (not long after I had tried to offer my life to God) and at the height of the disagreeing Mary Allen shook her head and said (as she had a thousand times) in that discouraged tone I knew so well, "Honey, you are *wrong!*"

Ordinarily this would have spurred me on to further justification of my point. But this time I stopped and thought about what she was trying to tell me. After a few seconds I said slowly, "Honey, I believe you're right. I think I *am* wrong."

Amazed, she looked at me cautiously to see if something sarcastic was coming; and when it didn't, she said, a little confused, "Wait a minute, maybe I'm wrong."

This may not sound like much to you. But it was the beginning of a whole new kind of life in the intimate soul of our marriage. For the first time I didn't need so desperately to be right . . . to be the victorious hero in all the encounters in our relationship. I could relax and begin to be myself. I suppose this new commitment idea I was trying to live would have been all right with my wife (she certainly liked some of the changes in me) . . . except for one horrible mistake I made: I tried to convince her that *she* should do the same thing. On the surface it sounds perfectly logical that a husband who has been deeply converted to a Living Christ should go about trying to get his wife equally converted. I am convinced that this is not only wrong, but that it is one of the unnecessary sources of deepest anguish in marriages in which only one partner is really trying to commit his or her life to Christ.

From *my* perspective I was trying to tell Mary Allen that I had found something wonderful—a freedom and sense of reality I'd never known was possible for people like us. But strangely, my most enthusiastic witnessing made her very cool and upset. I couldn't understand it. Later she told me that from *her* perspective all she could hear me saying those days beneath my words was that we had been happily married for five years and now suddenly I didn't like her as she was. I was not going to accept her fully anymore unless she *changed* into some kind of religious fanatic (or changed somehow in a way she didn't know how to change). I was threatening her very life and our life together . . . and of course I didn't even realize it, since I was saying such "good, true things." So, in her rebellion, she had begun subtly to point to areas in my life wherein if I were such a committed Christian, why was it that I "still reacted in the same old way?"

In my frustration I began to try to convince her that God had really changed me. In looking around for something to do to prove that I had changed, I did as many well-meaning Christians do when they are trying to convince someone close to them that they are different. I fastened onto something *I* liked to do. I decided to be more loving.

There is nothing wrong with being more loving . . . except that at the time it made me happier instead of her.

While I was looking around for some other way to convince my wife that I had really changed, my glance fell on the wastebasket standing full by the back door. "No, Lord," I groaned quietly to myself, "*Not* the wastebasket. Take my income, anything." But I suddenly knew that for me it had to be the wastebasket. Without saying a word I took it out, and didn't even mention it to her. (I had emptied it before in order to manipulate her into doing something I wanted to do. But not this time.) I began to really make an effort to take the trash out every day because I realized *that this was where my pride was fastened*. And I think this was when Mary Allen knew that something had really happened in my soul. I learned through this experience to look at the grubby little resentments and in areas where I am deeply defending my position to find really convincing ways to express the selfless love of Christ in my intimate human relationships with those people who truly know me.

Finally I realized the unchristian pressure my trying to force Mary Allen into my version of a Christian wife was having in her life. We were drifting further and further apart. Although things looked happy on the surface, we both knew that our marriage was bruised and broken on the inside where the world could not see. Finally one night I said to her, "Honey, I can't deny the tremendous things which have happened to me these past two years because of trying to give my future to the finding of God's will. But I have been wrong in trying to force all this on you. No one forced it on me. I'm sorry I tried (however unconsciously) to manipulate you by taking you to all these meetings, etc., to get you converted. I am really sorry." I went on to tell her, "When we got married I didn't sign up to *change* you, just to *love* you . . . and I do, just as you are."

This took the pressure off her, because I really meant it. Within a few weeks she went out and made a beginning commitment of her future to Christ all by herself, in the way which was right for her. (And it almost hurt my feelings that it didn't happen through me, but through a friend.) How wrong I have been so many times in these past few years in trying to change people instead of loving them. I believe we delude ourselves in thinking we can change people anyway. I am convinced that only God can convert anyone.

What happens when God's will becomes personally real and important to both partners in a Christian marriage? Then for the first time a Christian home is a live option. Now in the soul of our marriage it was not *my* vision of what a marriage or husband should be against *her* vision—one of us always having to be wrong. But now, together we began trying to find out Christ's vision of what our marriage should be.

Now that we both wanted a Christian home we began to try to live together in a new way. The awful sniping at each other wasn't as necessary to gain supremacy points or get even. We could often afford to admit we were wrong and help and accept each other with all of our faults, because we began to feel deeply accepted by God, even though we were seeing our selfishness more and more as we looked toward Christ.

For the first five years of our marriage I had been trying somehow to prove to Mary Allen that I was a "man"; and finally I could admit (she already knew, of course) that I am only a little boy trying to impress the world that I am a man. At last we could relax and begin to be children in the soul of our marriage and hope to find peace together.

All of this does not imply that a Christian marriage is one with no problems or even a marriage with fewer problems. (It may well mean *more* problems and some Christian marriages won't make it.) But it does mean a life in which two people are able to accept each other and love each other in the *midst* of problems and fears. It means a marriage in which selfish people can accept selfish people without constantly trying to change them—and even accept themselves, because they realize personally that they have been accepted by Christ . . . by God. And they are involved together in the adventure of trying to find God's will for their lives.

In honesty I must say that I am still an egoist and still a coward; but now, because of God's amazing gift of his presence and the perception which comes through beginning to give one's life to him with no strings, I can sometimes live and make decisions in my own personal life as if I were not these things. And believe me that is Good News!

MEMORANDUM

TO: Bruce

FROM: Keith

RE: Chapter 6, The Family

My part of this chapter seems to deal with the marriage problems caused by preconceptions and selfishness. Why don't you put in something you've written about the specific kinds of agonies that take place which make marriages split? What kinds of resources are available for married people who want to love God and each other in a more freeing and wholesome way?

Also, it seems to me that our kids take an awful beating when we parents are hammering out our relationships. Can you put in something about dealing with the roles of Christian parents in trying to relate in a vulnerable, honest way to our children (while getting to know God and each other)?

K.

❖ A FINE YOUNG ENGINEER I KNOW, IN THE process of discovering a Christian marriage, said, "Marriage is wonderful, but it doesn't solve all of your problems." I don't think it is supposed to! If you are unhappy before you marry, you will certainly be unhappy after you marry. Two people combine their problems when they marry, and living becomes even more complicated.

Christians believe that God intends marriage to be a wonderful, satisfying, and joyful relationship and that he has the power to make it so. And yet a truly happy marriage is not a common thing. Most of the marriages that fail never reach the divorce court.

We are surprised when a marriage "suddenly" breaks down. We are like the middle-aged man who began to lose his hair. Finally he had only one hair left on his head. He faithfully oiled and massaged that single hair. One morning he got out of bed and there on the pillow lay his one hair. With great anguish he cried out, "Great scott. I'm bald!"

Marriage does not fail because one of the partners suddenly finds someone else who is more interesting. It is *because* the marriage relationship had already broken down that one of the partners began to look elsewhere.

No change in our circumstances is going to solve the basic problem in our marriage. A better house, more money, moving away from the "in-laws," or being able to have children or sending the children off to camps and schools will not really change a thing. We must become aware of the underlying causes of unhappiness that drive our partners to infidelity or alcohol or any of a hundred kinds of escape.

What is a Christian marriage? Basically it means that I can no longer do as I please. In too many marriages one or both partners do just exactly as they please and wonder why things aren't better.

This self-will can take many forms. It can be expressed as hostility. We resort to nagging or irritability or actual fighting with our spouse. Being afraid to face the genuine cause of a failing marriage, we choose certain areas for battle. We fight about where to squeeze the toothpaste tube, how to discipline the children, who spends the most money foolishly, why the house is not better kept, and whose habits make them "just like" their mother. Such fights give us a chance to express our hostility without getting into the deeper and more painful issues.

It ought to be said at this point that, when there is open hostility, we can assume there is still caring. The situation is more serious when a husband or wife does not even care enough to fight or get angry, and instead says, "You go your way and I'll go mine." In such a marriage a man recently told me that his wife seemed more like a college roommate.

When God is allowed into the lives of one or both of the people in a marriage, we see that the cause of unhappiness is within the individual. It is the feeling that we are not appreciated enough, that we give more love than we receive.

I talked with a couple recently about their marriage. The wife said, "But I always give in. I wish just once *he* would give in. If he loved me as much as I love him, he *would*." This is the basic frustration in all unhappy marriages.

It has been said that when two people marry, they become one, but the question often is, Which one? Visualize two solar systems trying to occupy the same space at the same time; two suns vying for center with planets orbiting around each. The result would be chaos and collision. The same is true of a home with conflicting centers and different interests whirling around each. In some homes such a situation is solved by everyone yielding center place to one. Then the home centers around the mother or father or a child. Peace reigns, but the price is frustration and humiliation. This kind of peace is not the Christian answer.

In Christian marriage Christ is the center, and husband, wife, and children can find their proper orbit around him.

Let us express this mathematically. In a marriage without Jesus Christ, one plus one equals two. Where there are children, one plus one plus one plus one equals four, and four centers in a home are hell!

The Bible says about marriage, "These two shall become one." Mathematically this means that one plus one equals one. This sounds ridiculous in the science of mathematics, but it makes wonderful sense in the metaphysics of matrimony!

One attractive young couple came to realize that their budget was their biggest problem. Each felt that their tight budget and growing debts were the result of the other's irresponsibility and poor management. The subject was explosive and neither dared bring it up, knowing the violent consequences. The wife expressed her rebellion by going on a periodic clothes-buying spree, while the husband bought model trains.

When they admitted as new Christians that Christ could help them decide how they should spend their income, they were able in a short time to discuss their finances without anger, live within their income, and slowly begin to come out of debt. They set a time each week to go over the budget, and to remind them who had the final word, they always placed an empty chair at the head of the table.

Human love presupposes marriage to one's ideal. As disillusionment comes, the marriage breaks down. Christian love is not blind. It has its eyes wide open. It does not vanish when the other's faults appear. A Christian marriage involves seeing and understanding the other person as he or she really is and loving him or her just that way.

Christ's plan for two people who are married and who live their lives in him is that the wonderful glow of the courtship and honeymoon will not only last but deepen. True romance may not begin until we find this plan.

I can think of a couple married thirty years who are discovering Christian marriage after a lifetime of bickering and fighting. Today they are living in the glow of what it means truly to love each other. They are grandparents and also have young children of their own who share this new love in the home.

It all began with a conversation in which the wife expressed her lifelong complaint. Her husband was hard to live with and touchy. He sulked and was unreasonable. He was extremely stubborn. Above all, *she* was active in her church and her husband was not. She wanted to know how to make her husband a Christian!

It was pointed out that if she were really a Christian, her only obligation was to make her husband happy, not good. This was a new thought. She saw that in spite of all of her church work, perhaps she had never let Jesus Christ become the center of her life.

One day she made a list of all the things she knew should be different in her life. Then she prayed, asking God to come into her life and change all these things. She discovered a wonderful new peace.

Before long her husband, amazed by the change that had come over his wife, honestly faced the things that were wrong in his life. He prayed, asking Christ to forgive him and to take over his life.

There is no way for God to change a marriage and leave the people involved unchanged. C. S. Lewis said, "No clever arrangement of bad eggs ever made a good omelet." We waste too many of our prayers praying for the other person to change, when some really honest prayer for ourselves may do wonders.

Not long ago a woman came to her minister, begging him to tell her what to do with her alcoholic husband. She had taken all the abuse and humiliation and poverty she felt she could stand as the result of his drinking. Her minister asked her what she had done to try to change him. She said she had begged him, argued with him, shamed him, preached at him, read the Bible to him, threatened him, and prayed for him for years.

"Have any of these seemed to work?" the minister asked.

"No!" said the woman. "They have not."

"There is one thing you haven't tried. Why don't you pray for *yourself*, instead of your husband, and ask God to change all the things in your life that you know are wrong?"

The woman tried it and it worked. Her husband stopped drinking. He no longer had to escape.

I believe that almost anyone can discover a Christian marriage who will sincerely pray the prayer, "Lord, change this marriage beginning with *me*."

For those of you who are parents, this same kind of prayer can be the beginning of a new relationship with your children. Years ago when our son's Sunday school teacher asked the class of four-year-olds who God was, his hand went up. "God is a great big Presbyterian minister," he said.

While his response caused a good many chuckles in our congregation, it is not really an unusual one. Most young children have a hard time differentiating between God and their parents. This realization is enough to frighten the wits out of any conscientious Christian parent. After all, who of us by our actions wants to be responsible for God's character and reputation in the eyes of our children?

Since that time a quiet revolution took place in our home. Our daughter and our two sons are able to distinguish between God and their parents. Very simply, my wife and I stopped being our children's priests who heard their prayers and confessions, and prayed for their well-being. We still did those things, but we also confessed our sins to God in the presence of our children and, with them, received his forgiveness.

You can see immediately what happens. God is no longer someone in league with harassed parents, used by them to keep children in line. He is not the property of parents, a kind of grown-up secret, like Santa Claus. Rather, he is God of both parent and child, before whom each member of the family is responsible.

If I were to say that this "revolution" had not cost me a great deal in the way of pride, I would not be telling the truth. And, in spite of the fact that "losing face" is a small price to pay for a new and deeper relationship to my children and our deeper relationship to God, I am still constantly tempted by pride to "save face" and play priest when trouble arises in which I am involved.

It costs a great deal for a parent to worship God with a broken and contrite heart in the presence of his or her children, but I thank God that he has helped me to begin. I wouldn't live any other way.

But it should be said that some parents don't need to be broken and humbled. Rather they need to be starched and strengthened.

Some time before I started writing these observations I had lunch with a businessman from Texas, whom I'll call George. "What is the most exciting thing that God is doing in your life now?" I asked him, knowing that he had begun the Christian life some five or six years ago.

He pondered for a moment and then said, "I'm not sure I can explain it, or that you will understand or even appreciate it. The fact is, all my life I have been known as a 'good guy.' Everybody thought of me as 'good old George.' Even my family thought I was soft and easygoing.

"Well, since I have discovered the reality of Jesus Christ and God's love for me, I realize that much of my being a good guy has been weakness, and a desire to be loved because I was insecure. Now I find that Christ is giving me the freedom to lay down rules for my family and to back them up."

"What does your family think of you now that you are no longer a 'good guy'?" I asked George.

"It's the most amazing thing," he answered. "They all like the new me! I think my sense of authority, and the fact that I am taking spiritual and moral leadership in my home, has given them rules and structures that they have needed for growth and maturity. It has brought my wife and my children and me all closer together."

I told George I could appreciate what was happening to him and suggested that there is a unique shape of salvation for each of us. Jesus Christ saves us from all kinds of traps and pitfalls and wrong thinking about ourselves . . . so that we can love those entrusted to us with a more complete and liberating kind of love.

CHAPTER SEVEN

❖

JOB, SCHOOL, AND NEIGHBORHOOD

MEMORANDUM

TO: Bruce

FROM: Keith

RE: Chapter 7, Job, School, and Neighborhood

As I first began to wake up to the fact that Christian commitment wasn't synonymous with "going to church," it started a chain reaction of surprises. As I've said, I began facing the fact that God might want me to be a better husband and father, but it still didn't hit me that he wanted anything out of me in my vocational life except honesty and hard work.

I remember your saying once that one's work and faith are not only interrelated but that the attitude a Christian has about work is an interesting and very real barometer of that person's faith. How about discussing what you think a Christian should (or could) feel about his work as it relates to his commitment to God? (Maybe some specific guidelines?)

K.

❖ I'D SAY THAT IF YOU ARE MISERABLE OR bored in your work, or dread going to it, then God is speaking to you. He either wants to change the job you are in or—more likely—he wants to change you.

Remember the story about the blind man whom Jesus healed? After our Lord touched his eyes, he asked the man what he saw. He reported that he saw "men as trees walking." When he had received a second touch from the Master, he saw men clearly. I suspect that many of us need a "second touch" by Christ to see our jobs in their right perspective.

A friend in Illinois had joined a small group of seekers meeting for prayer and Bible study and the sharing of their faith each week. Although he had come a long way in his Christian commitment, each week he complained about the customers in his store—how unfair they were, how demanding, and how they took advantage of him.

But one day this man received a "second touch" by God and began to see the people who came into his store, whether to buy a package of nails or a washing machine, as people sent by God. He anticipated each sale as an adventure in personal relationships.

At Christmastime, with all the rush of increased sales, this man said to the group one night in amazement, "You know, what surprises me is how the people in this town have changed. Last Christmas they were rude, pushy, and demanding, but this year I haven't had a difficult customer in my store! Everyone is understanding and trying his best to cooperate." They all laughed. They knew the change had not been in the town but in the storekeeper.

But in a more profound way, perhaps the change was also in the town. As we see people through the eyes of faith, they actually do change. They respond to us almost directly in proportion to the amount of love we have for them as people.

Let me suggest five questions each of us might periodically ask ourselves about our jobs.

1. *Why am I here in this job?* Do you feel you are in your present job because of an accident? Because you happened to answer an ad, or your brother-in-law got tired of having you sit around and found you a job? Because of ambition? These attitudes certainly undercut any sense of Christian vocation. I think we should feel we are in our work because God has called us to do it, in just as real a way as he has called any bishop, clergyman, or priest.

Several months ago a man asked me to call on him in his large office in New York City. He said, "A year ago I turned my life over to Jesus Christ. It happened in my church." He then described the change that had begun to happen in his home—new communication between him and his wife; deeper understanding of his teenage daughter. There were many other evidences of his new commitment.

Then he said, "I find now, a year later, that I am still behind the same desk doing the same job in the same way, and I suspect something is wrong. If Christ has come in as Lord of my life, things should be very different in what I do here eight or ten hours a day." He was right, of course. Now he is exploring, along with some other men, the opportunities and approaches to Christian ministry in daily work.

We must dispense with the myth that commitment to Christ means becoming a clergyman or that work done inside a church building or in a church organization is more holy, somehow, than work done in the marketplace. Christ came to give us a sense of calling in everyday work. This is where the world is changed, and where the Kingdom is built.

Jesus himself was a workingman, and he called twelve workingmen to be his initial disciples. He might have been born into a priestly family, but he was not. We must understand the really radical thing God has demonstrated in Jesus Christ—that a new world and a new Kingdom can be built primarily through committed working people.

2. *For whom am I working?* Are you working for God, or for people? You cannot really serve both. When we are addicted to praise and thanks and rewards, we are in a real way under the tyranny of people and are working for them.

Often I feel sorry for some of the housewives and househusbands in the world who work long hours doing dreary housework. If they are working for the appreciation and thanks of their families, they seldom or never get it. But when we work for God, we are free to serve others no matter how unreasonable or thankless they may be. Our reward is God himself saying to us, "Well done, good and faithful servant."

We are even free to risk our job and the security of it if need be to be obedient to his will. If it is God to whom we are responsible, and from whom we get our reward, we are then free to be his people in any given situation.

3. *What am I working for?* Wages? Prestige? Or am I working to do the will of God?

An event from Christ's own life gives us insight. When he found people abusing others in the temple, he came in and violently upset the status quo. But when people wished to destroy him, he let them drive nails into his hands. Perhaps this is the kind of freedom Christian men and women need in their jobs:

not to strive for self-preservation to protect their own interests, but to look to the interests of others. This freedom comes only when we can answer the question, "What am I working for?" with "To do the will of God."

Where is your security? Is it in the person who pays your salary or can you see that person as an agent through whom God at this time has chosen to supply your needs? You cannot really love your boss or paymaster until you see that person as God's agent. If you see him or her only as your provider, then it is difficult to be honest with him, and fear and resentment are bound to color your relationship.

I have a wonderful Chinese friend, Moses Chow. His father had become a Christian in pre-Communist China and was told by his parents that if he persisted in following this "new god," he would be disinherited.

There was wealth in the family, but Moses's father could make only one choice, the choice of the new life he had found. So, he was disinherited and also left China.

Moving to a new home in the Far East, he became a very successful businessman. He left the security of the world he knew and trusted God, who was able to provide. Meanwhile, in the Communist upheaval in China, the family there lost everything. As Moses told this story of his father, it seemed to reinforce what I know has been true of my own life. When we are free to let go of the security of the world and trust God, he is able to provide. We don't follow God *because* he makes us secure, but if our security is in God, I believe he will provide even in economic matters.

4. *With whom am I working?* God seems to want us always to be aware of the people next to us. It's not enough just to work honestly and industriously, for Christ calls us to be a priesthood

of believers who willingly take responsibility for those who are our neighbors.

A railroad engineer came to his minister and asked to be put to work as a new Christian. The minister told the engineer that there was no position in the church open at the present time, but he said, "I do know of a job that only you can do—is your co-worker a Christian?"

This is the concept of the priesthood of believers. Our primary job is not to be an elder, deacon, or vestryman in the church, but to be a priest to the man next to us in our daily work. This is where we need to recapture the vision of the priesthood of the laity.

5. What kind of place am I in? Jesus Christ called us to be a part of a revolutionary movement. Because of this, the place we are in assumes tremendous importance.

Even a chambermaid making beds in a hotel can influence guests who go out and make decisions of worldwide importance. I believe Christians need to ask God for his strategy for the particular store, shop, industry, or service which is theirs. How could that particular organization be a part of his plan to change the world?

One day I was riding in a bus down Michigan Avenue in Chicago when an advertising poster attracted my attention. It was not a commercial message, and there was no indication of who had placed the ad in the bus. This is what it said:

My worth is not adequately recognized. Send a signal of fellow-feeling.

Today I did a foolish, embarrassing thing. Send a signal of shared chagrin.

My self-esteem is willing to trample yours. Send a signal of forgiveness.

I am alone in a selfish, disinterested world. Send a signal of mutual humanity.

To receive the mind of Christ is to hear the world saying just such words. Whatever else the world may be, it is lonely, hungry, guilty, and eager to make contact with a human being who will listen and understand, accept and love. The Christian should be just this kind of person. He or she ought to affirm that those outside of Christ have worth, uniqueness, and significance. The Christian can then affirm all of the deep human desires and longings that are in the world, call them good, and respond as a fellow human to a fellow human.

Jesus Christ himself is the pattern of this new kind of being turned loose in the world. We who belong to Christ ought to follow his example of love and affirmation for those who are outside the Kingdom, hoping that some will be affirmed to such a degree that they will themselves discover Christ and God's love in Christ, and thereby step inside the Kingdom.

Instead, it seems to me, we tend to emulate John the Baptist, calling down wrath and doom upon a lonely, lost society. Jesus loved John, to be sure, and called him the greatest of those born among women—but he added that John was "the least in the Kingdom of God."

It is easy to castigate the world, to catalog its sins. Easy, yes, and it doesn't cost us a thing. But Jesus Christ calls us to do the costly thing: to speak the word of love and affirmation for his sake.

For many years I commuted into New York City from my home in New Jersey. The trip involved a change from a Central Railroad of New Jersey train to a Path train, which is simply a subway connecting the two states. Squeezing into the overflowing car, I was shocked and astonished to hear a warm and friendly voice coming over the loudspeaker system, "Good morning! Welcome to the Path railroad!"

Those who live in the metropolitan New York area, and those who have visited recently, will realize how shocking it was to hear a warm and friendly greeting on a subway train.

I cannot remember all that the conductor said, but he was truly a pastor to a worried, harried, hurried bunch of commuters rushing into Manhattan. He had a friendly greeting at each stop, and as people left the train, he would open his window and call out a personal word to various ones whom he had come to know during his tour of duty on that line.

I could not resist going over and talking to that man. He told me that several years before he had had a real change in his life which had altered his whole life-style. Here was a man who was loving and caring for people as he daily conducted commuters into New York City. Certainly his witness has not been in vain.

New creatures in Christ, whether they be brain surgeons, teachers, farmers, or subway conductors, ought to be able to affirm the people who cross their paths or who partake of the services which they offer. I wonder how many people have spoken to that conductor, as I did, commenting on his friendly attitude and giving him the opportunity to bear witness to the source and motivation of his life-style.

But if the world needs to see Christians who are affirmative, it also needs to see those who are vulnerable. This is the other side of the coin of the Christian style.

Jesus himself could reveal his needs and hopes and fears to those about him. He was free to ask Zacchaeus for a meal and to ask a Samaritan woman of questionable morality for a drink of water. He was free to ask for the ministry of comfort and conso-

lation from three of his disciples on the night before his crucifixion. "Come with me into the garden and keep me company,"
he asked, "while I pray and wrestle through the will of God for
me as I face tomorrow and all it may hold."

This was the Lord of Heaven and earth, speaking in all his
vulnerable humanity. What does it say to us who seek to minister
in his name? All too often we have hidden our loneliness, hurts,
and hungers from other people—afraid that if we let them know
that we struggle as they do, we will fail to uphold God's reputation!

Nothing could be further from the pattern Jesus gave us. In
point of fact, authentic leadership involves sharing your troubles
with people and thus encouraging them in their struggles. The
Christian who wants to provide leadership must be willing to
acknowledge his own growing edge: his needs, loneliness, or
failures as a Christian.

Perhaps it is within the church then that we should learn how
to become vulnerable, and we can then transfer that vulnerability
to the world in a life-producing way in our jobs and homes and
neighborhoods.

There is a revolution going on in the world. Jesus Christ himself is the leader, and when we accept him as our Lord, he calls
us into it with him. He needs us and I believe he wants us to see
our jobs with the eyes of faith and understanding as something for
more than a means of earning a livelihood. Our jobs are places
where, as revolutionaries, we help to accomplish his revolution
in the hearts and lives of men and women everywhere.

MEMORANDUM

TO: Keith

FROM: Bruce

RE: Chapter 7, Job, School, and Neighborhood

Here's the stuff. In thinking and writing about vocation, I realize that I have spoken mostly of those kinds of jobs which my life as a professional minister touches (e.g., shopkeeper, conductors, etc.). But many of the people who read this book may spend their time in business offices. And I've never really "been there" in terms of the ongoing life and pressures of the business world from the inside. There's no question in my mind that most Christians would think it plausible that lay people can affect other persons in a life-producing way if they are teachers or nurses or in some service job. But what does God have to do with a business office?

I remember that the first thing I ever read that you wrote (long before *The Taste of New Wine*) was a short article in which you were telling how strange it was for you when you decided to try to "take God with you" consciously to the office. I think it would be good if you'd put some of that material in here about your own experience as you tried it the first time.

B.

❖ It has never ceased to amaze me that we Christians have developed a kind of selective vision that allows us to be deeply and sincerely involved in worship and church activities and yet almost totally pagan in the day in, day out guts of our business lives . . . and never realize it. I came to see the appalling extent to which this can be true when after having done four terms of seminary work, served on the vestries of two churches, and taught a large Sunday school class, a man who had worked in the same (oil company) division office I had for over a year said one day, "Gee, Keith, I didn't know you were a Christian." This stunned me into realizing that although I had taken Christ by the hand and led him through one passage after another in the labyrinth of my soul, I had always left him at the parking lot when I drove in to go to my office in the major oil company for which I worked.

I prayed about this but couldn't imagine how I could witness for Christ in that particular situation. It wasn't that it was so awful. It was just that the language, the risqué stories, and the competitive atmosphere left no oxygen for the spoken gospel to live in. Besides, I had been pretty fast for years with little suggestive innuendoes and an occasional profane outburst. Sigmund Freud said, very perceptively I think, in his *A General Introduction to Psychoanalysis*, that these unchanged areas in our lives are like nature parks which the city fathers in large metropolitan areas fence off and allow to grow wild just as they always have, so the citizens will have a little piece of the old life to wander through to remember how it used to be.

I think this is what I have done with certain areas in my outward life. Certainly I have done so with areas of my inward thoughts, which I had walled off from the encroachment of the Holy Spirit so that I might leave them just as they always have been. This being the case with me, how was I, of all people, supposed to bring the Living God into my vocational situation?

But I could get no peace in my prayer time until I tried. One morning I arrived at work, went into my private office, and closed the door. I sat down and prayed that God would somehow let me witness for him that day. Within an hour I had chickened out and was my same old attention-getting self. I was very discouraged.

At this point I stopped. Since I wanted to be Christ's person and yet didn't feel that I could effectively (or perhaps safely) do it in this pagan atmosphere, I thought this must be a call to go back to seminary and become a minister. Frankly it would have been simpler in many ways since people *expect* a minister to talk about Christ. But because of family and financial obligations, an investigation seemed to reveal that further education was out of the question at that time. Intensely disappointed I sat in my office one day and consciously surrendered my vocational life to Christ. As I sat there alone, it was as if my eyes were opened for the first time to the situation as it really was. I realized that the stereotype I had carried in my mind all my life of the Christian minister had blinded me to the fact that God might want me to be his special representative in that office.

But I realized that I really didn't know how to "witness in my vocation." I guess I was afraid it meant getting a basket of tracts as some men do and wandering down the halls making people wish I would get fired so that they wouldn't have to dodge me and my Christian witnessing. This method has never seemed very effective when aimed at me in the past. As a matter of fact now that I was a Christian I hated to be identified with those men (many of whom I knew were fine Christians). It wasn't that what they *said* was wrong; but there seemed to be a cool superiority about their attitude toward us sinners that didn't smack of the love of Christ. I knew that the God who had touched my life had loved me *before* I came to him, just as I was in all my weakness. There had to be a different way for me.

But there was no trail to follow in this mission field filled with sharp sophisticated young men and women. I did not even know how to begin. To be honest, I was very reticent even to mention Christ's name to most of my associates. After several periods of frustration and procrastination, I decided to take Christ's Presence with me in my conscious mind clear through a day at the office. And this was the beginning. I soon learned that years of contrary thought patterns made it difficult to practice the presence of Christ between concentrating on business matters. I was convinced that the quality of my work would be an integral part of any Christian witness I might have, so concentration on work was even more necessary. I realized that rather than worry about thinking of Christ all day, a Christian businessman must commit a piece of work to God and then really concentrate *on the work*.

To remind myself of God's Presence I decided to pray every time I walked to and from the drinking fountain down the hall. Things began to happen. As I walked through the offices and spoke to people, I was praying; and I began to pray for *them*. Although I could not notice any outward difference in my own attitude, some of the love and concern I began to feel for these people must have communicated itself to them, because without my saying anything about my new intention in that situation, people began to come into my private office and talk to me about their inner lives. I soon realized that behind the smooth, sophisticated faces in that company were many frustrated, lonely, and often frightened "little boys and girls" reaching out in the darkness of their souls for some meaning, some purpose in life. I began to see the extent of the need for Christ in the lives of "successful" people.

Before long I went to work for another company which was growing at a rapid rate. Another member of the management team there was a concerned Christian, but he too was stumped by the problems involved in trying to bring Christ consciously and effectively into a dynamic, hard-hitting, and very competitive business situation. We prayed together about it.

One Friday, when the executive vice-president was on a trip around the world and the pressures began to build because of critical business growth, I called my secretary into my office. "Lottie," I said, "I need to pray about this business. Monday morning I am going to come to work a few minutes early and pray in the conference room. If anyone else would like to do this too, they can."

I then went around to the department heads and secretaries and told them the same thing. This sounds very easy as I write it, but it was one of the most difficult things I had ever done in business. That weekend I kicked myself clear around the yard as I mowed it. Now, I had gone too far. It wasn't *my* company; and besides when no one showed up on Monday morning I would lose face as a manager. But I told God I was sorry for my lack of faith, confessed my self-centeredness, and said I was willing to fail for him . . . I thought.

The next Monday morning almost all of the fourteen people in that office were in the conference room. I realized then that many people really want God to be a part of their vocational lives, but there is no feasible corporate trail to follow. We decided that if God is real enough to be in Christ, there must be an intelligent way to allow him to become part of the situation of which we were a part. If not, he was too small to be God. We decided to pray for one another and for the people who came into that office, and we asked Christ to come into that company's life through us if it was his will.

This group was made up of people of very diverse religious backgrounds. There were a Presbyterian, two Roman Catholics, an honest agnostic, several Baptists, an Episcopalian, and one man who was studying Buddhism. We began to know each other on a different level. I began to love some of the ones I had only passed in the halls before. One day the man whom I felt was an agnostic, particularly concerning the person of Christ, came rushing into my office right after lunch and flopped down in a chair, looking very pale. That morning we had been talking about the fact that the Christian life and faith in Christ can only truly be grasped experimentally, through a committing of one's life. This had been hard for this man to see. He had an excellent academic mind. His father was an outstanding professor in biology at a Big Ten university. The young man had received a degree in chemistry and a graduate degree in geology with excellent marks. This idea of the *faith* in Jesus Christ having to come *before* the understanding sounded like intellectual suicide to him.

Now he was sprawled in a chair across from my desk staring at the floor. Finally he looked up and said, "Do you know what just happened to me?"

When I said I didn't, he related this story: It seems that on the way back to the office from lunch he had been driving in a crowded section of the city. Several cars ahead of him, a young mother had gotten out of a parked automobile and stepped backward right into the path of a truck, which struck her down. It all happened so quickly as he was inching toward the place where the woman's body lay that all he could remember was seeing the look of terror on the three-year-old little girl's face as she stared down at her mother through the open car door. A policeman had rushed up from the corner and was waving traffic around the accident. As my friend drove by, the dying woman looked up at him sort of pleading . . . and then disappeared from his view as he was motioned ahead in the traffic.

The shock of this incident had made a profound impression on the man opposite me in the chair. It had shattered the shell of intellectual sophistication, he said, inside of which he had been living. It had revealed to him starkly his mortality, and the truth that his real objections to committing his life to Christ were not intellectual at all. They were volitional. He simply didn't like the idea of giving up his will to God or anyone else. And upon realizing this, as he had driven on down the street, he had suddenly known existentially who he was and who God was. In the same moment he wanted deeply to respond to the Christ whose presence and love he now sensed in his own experience. Right there in the car he had consciously committed as much of himself as he could to as much of Christ as he could perceive. He prayed that God would come into his life and reveal himself more completely.

Needless to say this man's deep conversion, the subsequent newness of life, and sharing with him the thrill of new discovery had a profound effect on several of us. We realized that it had taken place in an atmosphere of love and acceptance over a period of months in the office.

I cannot say that what happened because of our meeting together made the company a lot of money. I cannot even say what the real effect on other people's lives was. I don't know. But the effect on my own was amazing. I saw that it was difficult for a man to swear at one he has just prayed with. I saw that both the women and the men in an office have a feeling of being a real part of a living company of people when they have prayed for the direction of their mutually shared vocational life. People began to treat each other more like people. This was true even though everyone was having to work under an unusually heavy schedule at that time.

People began to come into our offices, sit down, and say, "What kind of deal is this—these people laugh as if they were really happy." Together we began to learn to witness, to pray, to communicate what was happening in our lives to our wives, families, and our ministers, learning to adjust to the problems of office situations as Christian businesspeople. We had small groups of men coming to our offices to meet once a week to discuss the problems we faced in trying to be God's people in business. We would have sandwiches and discuss the Bible and its authority and relatedness to the new challenges we now saw all around us.

As we struggled with our own problems and those of the Christian businesspeople we knew, we found that it is not easy to take Christ into one's business as Lord. And I realized that what we were trying might not be best for any other company offices. Also we soon realized that we had to work harder than our non-Christian competitors and do a better job at our business, because we had to give up the "leverage" of cutting corners (in the inevitable dishonest practices in business and taxation procedures today). This may cost some money . . . a great deal of money.

People misunderstand your message. We found with Alfred North Whitehead that, "The success of language in conveying information is vastly overrated. . . . Not only is language highly elliptical, but also nothing can supply the defect of firsthand experience."[1] We came to realize that in the long run in our vocation the only real witness that would last was not what we *said* about our beliefs but what people saw us to *be*, week after week, in our dealings with our associates and our competitors. This was not a glamorous witness, and we made many serious mistakes. We were horrified as we began to see our real business personalities revealed. We were honestly astonished at our continuing selfishness and greed. Often we could only see our failure to witness. But with all of the difficulties, we found that we were experiencing the greatest life we had ever known. We saw the lives of some intelligent, seeking people in our vocational world changing before our eyes. Although we failed in many ways, we found ourselves a part of a Purpose, a Challenge that transcended the oil business.

Gradually, we began to discover a new sense of freedom from the terrible responsibility to be successful in business *or* in spreading the gospel. The *outcome*, we realized, was God's business. Ours was to do the "specifics" before us that day. Life began to be a different experience. We did not need to pressure anyone to accept God's Gift of himself. The "inner tracking" and actual converting could only be done by Christ. At last I understood what Karl Barth meant when he said about the Message: "I am glad I did not invent it, and hence it is not my responsibility to defend it. My only task and privilege is to tell you that God Himself said so and says so until this day."[2]

We discovered that it was fun (though painful) to try to be honest with one's self. We found that it was appalling to discover the extent to which we deceived ourselves in our vocational lives. We found it crushing to be misunderstood as a Christian. But transcending all these things, there was an inexpressible joy in sharing the experience of a businessman as he begins a new life and of watching him begin to live that life for God. But the real revelation I think we found in trying to take Christ with us into our business lives was that the further "out on a limb" we seemed to be going to try to be obedient to Christ's will as we could perceive it, the more *real he* became. This led to the realization that Christ does not promise the businessperson great material success in his or her vocation (though this may take place), but rather Christ brings the *inner security* which one seeks through great material success . . . and having found this, the burden of succeeding may be lifted. And this inner security is discovered in the day-by-day relationship with him.

What might happen to other people or groups who try to make their vocations Christian vocations? I do not know; but I think Dietrich Bonhoeffer came close to the answer when he said, "And if we answer the call to discipleship, where will it lead us? What decisions and partings will it demand? To answer this question we shall have to go to Him, for only He knows the answer. Only Jesus Christ who bids us follow Him, knows the journey's end."[3]

But we do know that it will be a road of learning and growing and of boundless forgiveness and mercy. And as a businessman I am very thankful for that.

CHAPTER EIGHT

❖

THE CHURCH

MEMORANDUM

TO: Keith

FROM: Bruce

RE: Chapter 8, The Church

Why is it so hard to look at "the church" honestly? As you know, I love the church and am glad that I am an ordained minister. But for years if I saw what seemed to be a serious mistake being made by church leaders, I felt disloyal somehow if I talked about it. And that's strange, because in every other area of life I had been trying to be honest with people, realizing that real honesty about a situation is the first step toward growth. I guess I felt guilty as if "who am I to criticize God's church?" But then I realized that we *are* his church. And what we say about the way our sin has allowed us to hurt people and build idols out of our structures and liturgies *is a confession* that *we have sinned* and are praying for a new chance at authentic *life in church!*

I've never talked to you much about this, Keith, but I know that you went to seminary and yet chose to remain a layman. So I know you've wrestled within your own life about the institutional church. How would you feel about including something you've written concerning questions like: Is it possible to accept God and not the church? What is the church primarily? (institution? movement? group? somehow a part of God?) How did you face these issues as a new Christian?

B.

❖ HAVING SEEN THAT LIFE WITH CHRIST CAN be real and that a Christian can face the present and begin to learn to love other people personally and responsibly, I began to hope that this might become the experience of the modern church. I started to examine my life in the institutional setting of the church. I had put this off for years and pretended that everything was "all right" about the church. I would say things like: "There are just different ways of being God's people," and of course there *are*. But in my case this statement was a dishonest evasion of the problem of facing my own relationship with that branch of the church to which we belong. I realized that for many years I had been inwardly sick of the church's programs. But I had also supported these programs by my gifts, my vote, and by my presence when required. Many times as a layman and as a businessman I have wanted to shout out in vestry meetings, "Friends, we are not doing anything which is relevant to anyone's *real* needs—*even our own. We are just keeping the church machine going because . . . well, because we don't know anything else to do!* For God's sake, let's take a new look at what we are doing!"

But I never did shout it because members of the vestry are community leaders, people of responsibility; and they and I—and the minister—all sitting there so seriously, seemed to represent a sort of implicit unquestionableness about the fact that things *must* go on that way. Besides being personally afraid of their rejection of me as some sort of a young religious nut, I also had to admit to myself that I honestly could not think of any realistically constructive way to change the operation. Further, speaking out against the church's basic stance in America at that time was sort of like speaking against motherhood. So to assuage my cowardice and frustration, I voiced my opinions strongly on specific issues which cluttered our meetings—like whether we should have a Coke machine in the parish hall or put basketball goals on the parking area.

I now believe we spent so much time on such issues because we were a *lot* more clear about our economic orientations than our theological ones. I was always glad when my time to serve on committees was over. But in retrospect I found that in some cases everyone, including the minister, felt the same sense of frustration with the nature of the life we lived together in those meetings.

As a result of my first conscious attempt as an adult to make a commitment of my *life* to the Living God, I began to understand that God accepted me with all of my shortcomings, some of which I was now becoming secure enough to see. I became so excited about the new life I was finding that I had to speak out in vestry and committee meetings.

I knew that the meaning and purpose I had longed for were real and must be available to other people because *I was finding them*. Somehow *the church's program* should provide a way that this could happen to others who had become discouraged with life.

It was only when I began to suggest changing the church's program that I found out about conflict as a Christian. Because, when I spoke out, my ideas and enthusiasm were met with a sort of embarrassed silence. Suggestions I made were either subtly tabled, or I was made "chairman of a committee to investigate." When I did investigate and offered suggestions, I found that I had somehow gotten on a different communication frequency from most of the vestry members I knew. People simply did not see what I was now seeing. I could not blame them since I had spent years in the church and not seen that God could "come alive" to people like me and change the whole meaning of being a Christian. Since I did not know what to do in terms of a new program, I was very frustrated in church meetings.

The minister we had at that time was a fine man, but he had tried programs for years. And with all his efforts and integrity he had found no way to motivate people to get involved in these programs at more than a token level. He was tired. And now he was somehow playing the game with us, dutifully reminding us of our "spiritual obligations"—but basically, it seemed to me, thinking in terms of corporate business methods and results, though he did not know this since he had never been in a corporate business structure. But I began to realize that the problem was not primarily a disagreement about methods, as it seemed to be on the surface. Rather we had a much deeper difference—in our basic perspectives. We no longer meant the same things when we spoke of "the Christian life."

As I saw more clearly the sickness and self-centeredness in my own life, I also began to see the sickness and self-centeredness in our corporate church life. The difference was that, personally, I was becoming free to confess my phony ways, when I could see them, and find acceptance and forgiveness. And this was freeing me to take risks and, for the first time, to think creatively about relationships and purpose in church programs. Consequently, I began to shake off activities which, for me, were unreal. I saw that *life did not have to be the way it always had been*. My life was becoming an adventure. I became interested in people's needs and actually cared about some of them. But in the organizational life of the church, no one seemed to see that there was even anything wrong, much less that a *whole new experience of living was waiting just outside our humdrum life together*.

I made awful mistakes and unconsciously intimidated people by my implicit rejection of their faith and practice, as I tried to express mine. We were in several churches in different cities during that time. I taught Sunday school and began to try to communicate personally that which I was finding. But the more people began to believe what I was saying, the more trouble the church had. People whispered about "cliques" and "dangers." I began to see the terrible threat that the kind of meaning of the gospel I was finding can pose to those who are not finding a "new experience of life." Because, from the outside this "new" life looks like an emotional and socially naïve, nineteenth-century piety, which it usually is not.

I also saw how threatened I was at the church's rejection of that which was becoming increasingly real to me. I remember a prominent theological professor asking in effect, "Who do you people think you are to criticize the church when it has had two thousand years of corporate universal experience to its credit?" And I felt a little subdued. Who were we indeed? But I simply *could not deny what was happening in my life* and in the lives of those whom I now knew in many denominations. Their experience was so much like mine that I felt as if we were in the same family. And the spirit we were finding had the aroma of the New Testament Church about it. And the fruits were love and peace and creative purpose toward others. For the first time I could speak about the Christian life with a little authority, because I knew that life inside my own skin was different. But I began to feel that I was fighting a hopeless battle in trying to express this faith in my own church. And I could not for the life of me figure out why.

Gradually, the real focus of my Christian life moved away from the institutional program of the denomination to which we belonged. I found small but growing interdenominational groups whose purpose and witness clearly seemed to be to lead men and women into the new style of life I was finding. In the joy and acceptance of this exciting and open fellowship there was not time to worry about the problems of the institutional church. We were communicating with amazing ease in these small groups, and many of us were experiencing a real love for other human beings. Genuine transformations were taking place in behavior, attitudes, and relationships. People were being freed from alcoholism, families were being healed, and compulsives were finding peace. People flocked together in larger and larger local, regional, and even national meetings to share the insights, love, and adventure we were finding in our own small groups.

But the renewal movement was growing so fast that its energies had to be spent almost entirely on helping large numbers of new people to start learning the disciplines involved in living the Christian life. Those of us who were deeply involved emotionally or professionally in this movement found ourselves swamped with speaking engagements and with developing conference programs and techniques having to do largely with helping people to *begin* the "committed Christian life." Later we started helping those who had begun trying to live for God themselves to learn to help others begin. We made naïve errors and oversimplified many things. We had looked at the institutions' programs and found them mostly to be academically oriented and not psychologically practical in the threatening world of the laity.

After a few exhausting but exhilarating years, I stepped back and tried to see what had happened. It seemed to me that in one sense the "God is alive" Christians of America were divided roughly into two groups. On the one hand, there was a great and continually multiplying body of new or "renewed" Christians trying openly to commit their whole lives to God. This group's success numerically with getting lay people to *begin* a new life was in danger of causing us to produce a generation of highly motivated witnessing Christians who would only know how to live the *first year* of the Christian life. *

---

* During the year to which I am referring I was invited to several interdenominational meetings held for the purpose of learning how to live the Christian life. These meetings were organized and sponsored by ad hoc groups of lay people and were open to any interested Christians. Several hundreds of application letters were sent back from one three-day meeting because of lack of space. (Seventeen hundred people from almost every state in the Union did attend.)

In starting new small groups, the "older" Christians found themselves living their first year again and again with different people. Many of these group leaders have never had time themselves to penetrate the broad stream of our generation's corporate life and needs. They have never faced the *longer-range* personal problems involved in the living out of one's life in changing family and age situations. The new groups had the danger of replacing involved evangelical *living* in the real world with a continuous evangelistic *program*, which was a thing apart from the ordinary tasks and relations of secular life. It was an exciting but frothy life, and some of us yearned for the stability of the humdrum routine of living. We were caught up in a glorious treadmill of meetings and witnessing, which had become our lives.

On the other end of this religious spectrum there were the program people of the institutional church. Leaders in this group, who were often very suspicious of the new lay movement, were concentrating and redoubling their efforts almost entirely on religious education, corporate worship and responsibility, and social involvement. But these people seemed to be operating with the strangely blind assumption that laypeople in the church already have the kind of motivation to risk vulnerable involvement in the world—when they will not even support the church's basic internal program. And when their passionate pleading for involvement has met with stubborn silence, the resulting frustration in ministers' lives has been dreadful to behold. So as I looked

---

Hundreds of people were turned away from these meetings simply because the hotel accommodations were not available, and yet in almost no instances that I know about were there any promoting or advertising or any "expenses-paid delegates." Whatever one may say about the meeting content, there is little doubt that the participants were highly motivated. At least anyone who has tried to get a parish weekend conference together would tend to think so.

around, I saw those of us in the lay awakening concentrating so hard on the necessary "beginnings" we were starting to look to the rest of the church like a new and joyfully motivated nation of "spiritual midgets." And the institutional church, in its horror at what appeared to be an anti-intellectual renegade spirit, was concentrating so hard on "educating" people who had never been born that they were producing a grim and cynical company of "walking dead people." They were finding little of the winsome and motivating joy of living and loving which has always marked the Christian Way. And the lines of tension between these two groups had been drawn.

Many institutional church leaders have been deeply disturbed by the apparently self-centered "small groupism" and "happy talk" of the newly converted Christians. The new Christians, on the other hand, are appalled that the church's program has no way built into it to bring the people being ministered to into a personal reorienting relationship with the Living God and with each other—a relationship that is more than outward form. And neither side is attractive to the other. New Christians ask me, "Why should I want to go back to the cold, rejecting, cynical church (which will not take me seriously as a person)?" On the other hand church leaders say about the new group: "Can't they see that their lives are being lived in an unreal cocoon—that they must burst out into the world to be fully Christ's people?"

But the baffling part of this separation is that many members of *both* groups think that they have *already been on the other side and that the other side is a blind alley.* For instance, many of the education-social involvement people have rebelled against a childhood in the midst of inflexible legalistic men and women who had claimed that all you have to do is "give your life to Jesus" and you are in—you are safe and free from the awful, sinful world. On the other hand some of us who were raised in a liberal, pragmatic atmosphere tried to "do good works," and life was really no different for the people we helped. We just frustrated them by giving them a clearer vision of what they did not have. Our good works just put Band-Aids on cancers and either made us feel superior (at least we were doing something) or left us disillusioned, or both. And the people's lives were not changed so that they could creatively help themselves. But now it seemed to me that the truth was that both sides had correctly pointed out the dangers of the other's stance, while *missing* the essence of the other's reality—the lack of which is blocking both factions in their struggles for wholeness under God.

When I began to see the extent to which both groups were right in their criticisms of each other, I knew that the time had come for me to take a step. This was when I thought of turning back to the church and coming home emotionally to its life. I had seen literally hundreds of men and women, many of whom had never been active in the church, come alive and begin finding purpose, direction, and personal involvement in their own worlds. But who was going to take them to raise? At conferences we could give them materials and suggestions on how to get started. But we knew that if they were to discover their own place, the unique form of their obedience in the world would have to find a group with lasting continuity in their own community. This would have to be a continuing fellowship in which they could learn to walk through the tragedies, changes, and inevitable human encounters through the years. Such groups could provide centers of hope in different communities, as Paul's groups did in the early church—small centers through which people, as seriously and personally committed Christians, could come to grips with the problems of their lives and the screaming issues of our time.

When I looked back at the church, it was with a feeling of

ambivalence. On one hand, I felt a vague repentance for the immature and defensive scorn I had felt. But on the other hand, I now had a calm realization that many of the ministers and lay people in the church simply cannot imagine the nature and extent of the "grass roots" reformation taking place all around us. They cannot see from the outside the power, hope, and integrity being generated in the lives of growing thousands of people. I saw that the church cannot be the church without a company of men and women with drastically changed purposes and directions, deeply motivated to be a servant people devoted to their Lord. But I also saw that the evangelical awakening cannot become a mature reformation until it leads people into the brokenness and alienation of the secular world. The only two alternatives I could see for me were: (1) to get *someone* to start another denomination, or (2) to get back to my own.

When I did start back, I learned a strange thing. For years I had been very suspicious of ministers because I had been deeply hurt by a few. I remember several years ago being asked to speak to an annual clergy conference in the diocese in which we lived. I came to the conference with some reservations. And as I looked around and visited with the ministers, I remember thinking, *What a hostile bunch!* I had the feeling that they really thought the lay renewal bit was naïve. After I spoke that evening, there seemed to be a much cooler atmosphere. I decided that they were after me. I cannot help smiling as I write this. Recently I addressed the men of the same diocese and many of the same clergy were present. I had to tell them that it had taken three years, and a year and a half of graduate study in psychology, for me to realize that it was *I* who was after *them*. And although I had not known it at the time, this was true. I had been so afraid of being rejected that I looked for—and consequently found—rejection coming from them. And of course some *was*. But what I did not see was that it was my suspicions and largely unconscious judgment of them that brought on a good bit of the lack of openness on their part. Since that meeting, several ministers have confessed the same experience from the other side of the issue—after realizing that their own unconscious rejection of new lay Christians, who have gotten "turned on" outside their program, has brought on much of the trouble they have had in their churches. (It is amazing how many more ministers I meet these days who are interested in the church renewal.)

Now I was beginning to see how both we on the "outside" in the lay renewal and those in institutional program groups had been telling the Lord that the other group's members had taken the first bite of the apple in the garden. But now I was starting back into the orchard.

Coming Back into the Church

In coming back to a more emotionally involved role in the institutional church, I had to take a new look at the old problems that had caused me to leave in the first place. I had never left physically, having belonged, attended, and given regularly to the church all along, but my real interest had left. The old problems I had seen were still there, problems like "Why is there so much confusion concerning what we are about in the life of the church?" And, "Why is it so difficult for us to really go out on a limb for the programs we do decide on in our church meetings?" It was not until just before "coming back" that I began to see what these problems have actually meant in my life.

I had been asked to speak to a group made up primarily of ministers in Boston. My job was to talk about how a layman can really be a Christian in the church, beyond attending the worship services. I was excited about going (Boston is a long way from South Texas), and I wanted very much to do well. But I could not prepare and kept putting it off. Finally, the day came when I *had* to sit down and write my talk. But I could not write. I sat at my desk, paralyzed, staring at the blank paper for almost an hour. I began to sweat. Perhaps nothing would come to me. But, while sitting there, I saw that I was facing my own question in a horribly real way. Here the church had given me an assignment in its program—an assignment I wanted to do. Yet, I still could not get myself off dead center to get involved. As I sat there, I asked myself "why?" What was on my mind that was keeping me from being engaged in the program before me? I began to examine my thoughts during the previous hour—and I was ashamed. Do you know what I had been thinking? On the same program of the session at which I was to address the conference there was to be another speaker. This man is a person whom I considered to be one of the most articulate and loving spokesmen for Christ in our time, particularly with regard to the problems of the laity. He was to *precede* me on the same platform without so much as a hymn between us, *speaking on the same subject that I was assigned*. I realized as I sat at my desk that what was going through my mind was the fear that *I might not look too good following Kenneth Chafin!*

Here I was, a consciously committed Christian, going fifteen hundred miles to tell a group of men about the freeing love of Christ. I could not prepare my address because my mind was occupied with how *I* was going to look. I tried to recall what else I had been thinking about during my hour of paralysis. I remember that I had been trying to figure out how I might capture these men's imaginations for Christ. This seemed much more noble than my previous thoughts until I had to ask myself, "Or do you want to capture them for yourself?" And, of course, I never did know for sure. But as I sat there I began to see something else. I realized that perhaps *here* was the critical problem, the reason I had not been able to really throw myself into the church's program: I had always had some much more fearful and threatening inner problems which had to be dealt with *before* I was free to even begin to be personally involved in the larger program of the church with integrity. And those personal problems and doubts made me very uneasy about speaking for the living Christ without being a hypocrite.

What has apparently happened is that those of us who have been in policy-making positions in local churches have made some very faulty assumptions about lay people and the church. We have assumed that their presence at vestry or deacons' meetings indicates a deep personal commitment to God and his purposes. We have assumed that these people have a freedom from self-centeredness and fear of other people's opinions. We have *acted as if we* believed that they are ready to go out and openly share the freedom and understanding of their faith (which they are presumed to have) if only we could come up with the right vehicle for them, the right program. *But it is not so!* At least for me and for dozens of others whom I have asked in moments of honest sharing, these assumptions simply *are not true.* Most of us had not been elected to vestries for qualities of dynamic personal and loving Christian involvement with people. Some were elected because of financial success. Others, the minister had asked to run. Some were elected to keep the "spiritual element" (or even the minister) from going off half-cocked. Many of these elected saw the vestry's function as a sort of financial advisory board to which the minister was to provide the spiritual direction (when there was time). For other vestrymen membership was an honor, like other civic honors.

Most of us did not have any clear, conscious picture of what it might mean for us to *really be* committed Christians in our world. And yet the ministers assumed that we were the spiritual center of the church. But the truth was that most of us did not even know what the central human problems of alienation are—to which the gospel might speak in the world. Because we did not know how to do that for which we were supposedly formed, we either became a rubber-stamp group whose main purpose was to get the meeting time shortened, or we had long arguments primarily over financial issues, in which the lack of real communication was at least notable. We were often very frustrated, because we could not even pin down our own basic problems and disagreements.

But if all this is even partly true, and a person is deeply interested, how would he begin to find out what the real problems are in the church?

About a year ago I was doing some studies in motivation and perception. And I began to realize that people do not necessarily respond to the facts before them, but rather they respond to what they *perceive* before them. And what I perceive *is* reality for me in determining my responses, even if my perception is *incorrect*. A classic example of what I am saying is the story of the two men traveling at night in the brushland of the Southwest. The driver lived on a ranch in the area, but the passenger was a stranger from the East. Suddenly, as they approached a cut through a hill the Easterner saw in the headlights a boulder rolling down into the road ahead of them. He yelled, clambered toward the backseat, and covered his face. The driver, on the other hand, drove on without a sign of any disturbance because he knew that the "boulder" was a tumbleweed. Both men had seen the same object, and both had reacted appropriately to what they saw. Yet one almost went into a spasm, and the other's blood pressure did not even change because one man had been living where he could see and handle tumbleweed, and the other had not.[1]

And I think this is what has happened in the whole business of church renewal in many cases: some ministers and church people have seen the restless stirring among laymen and the clamor for "change" and "honesty." But because of their past experience with cliques of gossips and malcontents these ministers may *perceive* unsponsored lay activities as irresponsible and almost go into a spasm at the perceived danger.

I have been frustrated for years in trying to understand the basic problems we have in local church programs because I have not known a simple fact about the way we, as people, solve problems—any kind of problems. For instance, imagine that you and I are assigned a simple problem in arithmetic to solve. Actually let us say that there are three of us. One of you is an ordained minister and the other a layman. I am standing before you with a blackboard behind me. On this blackboard I write with white chalk this simple problem: $\frac{9}{8}$. Then, let us say that I ask you to give me the first answer that pops into your head. When I actually did this, the minister came up with the answer "1." I turned to the layman and asked him what answer he got. Without hesitation he said "72." With the *same given information* the minister's and the layman's answers were 7,100 percent apart. What had happened? Both men laughed as they realized that one had unconsciously *assumed* that it was a subtraction problem $(9 - 8 = 1)$ and the other had *assumed* that it was a multiplication problem $(9 \times 8 = 72)$ although I had given *no* sign to indicate that it was either. And each was correct from his own perspective. Before one can solve any problem, he or she evidently brings from past experience an opinion or "mind-set" as to what the problem is. And that mind-set determines and limits the answer to the problem in a real way, even though the mind-set is usually unconscious or at least unexamined.

I believe that this is what happens to us in our church meetings, and even between denominations. These preconceptions cause a good bit of our uncanny frustration and discord. Each of us comes into such meetings with preconceived ideas about what it means to be a Christian, most of which are not even conscious. And these different ideas about what constitutes Christian living and purpose become the "signs" which we unconsciously affix to every problem. And these often buried ideas become the stubborn personal criteria against which we unconsciously check the items that come up for consideration.

When this hit me, I realized why it has been so difficult to communicate about the life-changing experiences many people are having in the church today. Although the stalwart churchman understands the *words* the new Christian uses to describe his or her new life, he sees in these words entirely different *meanings*. Without realizing it he has from his past put a negative "sign" on words like *conversion, witness, evangelism*. But the new Christian's "sign" is very positive regarding these terms. So, looking at the same word symbols, the two get totally different "answers" about the value of the experience described.* And this difference carries over into the conducting of church program-planning. Since we have not self-consciously examined these assumptions, for the most part, all we know consciously is that a proposed action "doesn't sound right to me." Yet we cannot give adequate reasons for our objections, so they sound like a personal rejection of the *person* submitting the plan. An argument ensues

---

* As Piet Hein, the Danish poet and scientist, put it in another context, "Ideas go in and out of words as air goes in and out of a room with all windows and doors widely open." *Life*, 14 October 1966.

in which our logical reasons often sound weak, even to us, but our stubborn sense of being right is very strong.

What then is the solution? In coming back into the problems of being identified with the church, I found that the thing that has helped me most is that during these past few years I have begun to become *conscious* of what I think it actually does mean to live and grow as a Christian. I have begun to believe that the Christian life is a *pilgrimage*, not a *program*; a pilgrimage with people who want to be willing to love, live, and possibly die for Christ, each other, and the world. I have begun to experience what it is like to take the risk of revealing *my* true needs, and to love other Christians enough to let them *help me* when I really hurt—as well as trying to help them. And built into this life is a yearning to share with others the freedom and healing one is finding. To know these things is giving a possible unity and direction to my whole life and to all the programs of the church in which I am involved. And when there are choices to be made about program, these criteria help me to evaluate where I should invest my time.

I'm beginning to believe that before we can formulate programs in the church which will affect anyone's real life situation, we will have to be educated in such an atmosphere that our inherited *perceptions* can change about the whole Christian enterprise. Somehow we must design Christian educational adventures in which we can investigate experimentally in the church what it may mean to be "committed Christians."

And the good news is that the winds of creative change are blowing in the church as 1992 is approaching. The 1990s have been declared "the Decade of Evangelism" by the Episcopal Church, and several other denominations have made this sort of commitment. Once again, new life is breaking out within denominational structures!

MEMORANDUM

TO: Bruce

FROM: Keith

RE: Chapter 8, The Church

You pulled my chain, and I'm afraid I've included more than you asked for (again). But I'm committed to the church too. And my heart aches at the way we often live as church men and women. Now that I am a "professional" communicator I have a good many of the same problems you pastor types have—even though I'm technically a layman. (So for some strange reason I'm not nearly as critical of professionals.)

But I don't think there is anything *absolutely sacred* about the church except its Lord, Spirit, and Father: *God.* Our programs and procedures in my opinion are to be judged by the biblical criteria of their "fruits." If healing, understanding, sacrificial living for others, and love are not resulting from our programs, I'm for trying to face our condition, confess our sins, and ask God to give us new forms and structures to experiment with.

It seems apparent to me that we are really phony and the world sees us only too accurately as a body of hypocrites. But I don't think that cynical, caustic, and critical "honesty" is the answer. Why don't you insert something at this point about the *kind* of honesty that might be appropriate in the church?

K.

❖ I'M CONVINCED THAT GOD IS NOT SHOCKED by our sins. I can't think of a single sin that any of us has committed, or is now practicing, that Jesus Christ did not deal with realistically in his life and sacrificially on the Cross. Jesus associated with call girls, alcoholics, and chiselers. He didn't condone what they did. Nor did he leave them as he found them. But the record indicates that they enjoyed his company.

However, it is recorded in the fifth chapter of the Book of Acts that two very fine people—Ananias and Sapphira—dropped dead in his first church. They weren't drunks. As far as we know, Ananias wasn't stepping out on Sapphira. They went to prayer meetings. They were more than tithers. But they were pretending something that wasn't true before God and his people. They didn't have to give a cent to the church from the land they sold, but they *pretended* to give it all when they actually gave only half.

Now God didn't kill them. The spiritual laws are such that when we are hypocrites, we cut ourselves off from the life God wants to give, and often we pick our own kind of death—a sudden coronary, as they might have had, or some slow death. But death is inevitable, whether physical, mental, psychic, or spiritual.

How accurate a picture do Ananias and Sapphira give us of our own lives and our own churches? Do I dare find out who I really am? Have I let anyone else know who I really am? The lie we live is probably only a lie we tell ourselves. Most people who get close to us surely see more than we think but are too polite to tell us what they see.

The neighborhood bar is possibly the best counterfeit there is to the fellowship Christ wants to give his church. It's an imitation, dispensing liquor instead of grace, escape rather than reality, but it is a permissive, accepting, and inclusive fellowship. It is unshockable. It is democratic. You can tell people secrets and they usually don't tell others or even want to. The bar flourishes not because most people are alcoholics, but because God has put into the human heart the desire to know and be known, to love and be loved, and so many seek a counterfeit at the price of a few beers.

With all my heart I believe that Christ wants his church to be unshockable, democratic, permissive—a fellowship where people can come in and say, "I'm sunk!" "I'm beat!" "I've had it" Alcoholics Anonymous has this quality. Our churches too often miss it.

The rebirth of a biblical theology in most of the major denominations today has resulted in a commitment-centered message. I genuinely rejoice in it, but it's not enough. One more altar call, decision card, church officers' retreat, or campfire surrender won't do it. Something else is needed. *A fellowship must exist where committed people can begin to be honest with one another and discover the dimension of apostolic fellowship.*

It is interesting to see that a large portion of the secular, indifferent, irreligious part of our society today often has more reality and genuine concern for others than many church people.

There is a minimum of soul-stifling pretense on the part of many pagans. They cheat on their income tax and laugh about it on the golf course. They get drunk in front of their whole club. They tell their marital troubles in detail to their hairdresser. They talk honestly to their bartender; they talk deeply to their psychiatrist; and they talk indiscreetly in the locker room to each other. But there is after all a real openness and transparency that is healthy.

We all know what can happen when one of these open, honest pagans comes to a Billy Graham meeting or some similar place and there is a chance "to make a decision." When the statement, "Jesus Christ, take my whole life" is coupled with their honesty, we see them born in the Spirit right before our very eyes!

Commitment alone does not open the door for the Holy Spirit to empower us and to do his desired work in us. A second key is needed. We can call it *honesty*—a word seldom found in a theological word book or concordance. The biblical word *confession* makes most Protestants today think of a little booth and a priest. I do not think this is what the New Testament writers intended. I believe they meant more people to be honest with God in the presence of others—and to be honest with each other.

For the committed Christian who has missed the power of the Holy Spirit to become a new person, honesty with another about himself can remove the blocks and bring freedom and release. The Holy Spirit can come in, do his work, and give his gifts. He does not have to be coaxed or implored. When we make the conditions right and remove the blocks, he is immediately free to heal and help and empower.

When God has his way and we are liberated, we know it and the world knows it. He doesn't make us perfect. We still have to say "forgive me" daily. But we "walk in the light" with God, each other, and ourselves.

Honesty is essential to Christian growth. God keeps showing me that at heart I am a phony (another name for a sinner). I used to tell out-and-out "social" lies, but I have gotten beyond that (restitution was too painful!). I am much more subtle now. I can lie with the truth. I can project an image which is all based on fact, but which gives a totally false picture about me, my family, my work, or my church. But when we live the honest, open life in apostolic fellowship, God's people puncture those lies. It is costly, but therapeutic and liberating.

Honesty is God's way for a family of Christians to become a Christian family. In our first church, after graduating from seminary, my wife and I were both committed Christians, but we hadn't yet discovered a Christian marriage. Two other young married women began to meet with my wife—both members of our church. Over coffee one morning the three admitted for the first time how they were failing as wives and mothers. When they prayed together, Christ's healing began.

We three husbands saw and experienced this change in our wives and soon there were six committed people trying to live in honest fellowship, meeting together each week. The group began to grow and divide. Inside of two years there were about a dozen groups like it meeting throughout the city, involving people from dozens of churches. But it all began when three women over coffee said, "This is who I really am. I don't want to be like this anymore. Jesus Christ, will you change me?"

Our children need to know who their parents really are. This can help give them freedom to minister to us. One of our sons, when he was six, prayed one night at family devotions, "Lord, forgive us for running all over the country telling people about Jesus and then being so grumpy at home!" They pray for us and become an instrument of Christ's healing. Their faith then is in Jesus Christ himself, not in a false picture of their parents' goodness.

Honesty is also a key to fellowship. One equation for New Testament Christianity is fourfold. "And they devoted themselves to the apostles' teaching and fellowship, to the breaking of bread and the prayers" (Acts 2:42). Most churches are strong on doctrine, prayers, and communion. But the apostolic fellowship is missing. This isn't the only way to the renewal of the church, but it's part of the whole pattern. A three-wheeled wagon can't go far. All four wheels are required for the church to be the Church.

Honesty is the key to personal effectiveness with people. God uses my confessed, redeemed sins more than all the theology and psychology I've learned. When I'm counseling just with sound biblical theology, I never see "biblical" results. The price needs to be paid in personal honesty.

The Bible is full of the theology of confession. It begins with Adam and runs through the institution of the Levitical priesthood, the experience of the psalmist, the conviction of the prophets, and on into the New Testament. Even church history tells us that the early church practiced confession within the fellowship for the first four hundred years. Confession to a priest became an option, and remained an option from the fifth century until a papal decree in the thirteenth century made it the only way. With the Protestant Reformation confession to God alone became the only way for many.

Today with the renewal of the church centering on the rediscovery of the lay ministry, small group fellowships are becoming honest and are beginning to face the burning social and political issues of our nation. We are beginning to see on a large scale new facets of the old truth that honesty is the *only* policy.

CHAPTER NINE

❖

BROKEN RELATIONSHIPS AND MORAL FAILURES

MEMORANDUM

TO: Bruce

FROM: Keith

RE: Chapter 9, Broken Relationships and Moral Failures

One of the first problems I faced (or rather *avoided* facing) in my relations in the church was a problem I've had in *many* relationships during my whole life. I am so insecure and have secretly had such low feelings of self-worth that when I have suspected someone was better than I at something we both did, I would subtly tear them down—thinking semiconsciously, I suppose, that in "correcting" them or pointing out their faults, I'd somehow build myself up. I always hate myself when I do this and often end up with an infected or broken relationship on my hands.

You helped me a lot with this problem, Bruce. Why don't you include something about a less phony Christian style of relating to the significant others in one's life? How do we become radically vulnerable and affirmative to those with whom we live? And how do we handle the bruised relationships we scatter along the way?

K.

❖ F<small>OR SOME OF US THE MOST DIFFICULT</small> thing in the world is to be affirmative to others. We are often tempted to feel that we must take God's place and play the corrector or the "straightener-outer" of someone else, rather than to bring to him or her the word of affirmation that would really make a difference in his or her life.

Let me speak for a moment as a husband, and as one who at times cannot bear to be outwardly hostile but must play some kind of "Christian game" even in anger, and withdraw into a shell of politeness. Suppose that you are such a husband, and that for several days and nights you and your wife have been withdrawn or hostile and your physical and verbal communication has been close to zero.

Then suppose that God finally gets through to you and tells you that life is too short to live like this; that you must seize the moment and love as God loves you. It is up to you to break the stalemate. Night falls, bedtime approaches, and you decide that the time has come to reestablish communication with your wife.

As a husband, you have two choices of what to say: both true, but both only half-truths. You may smile expectantly and say with as much warmth as possible, "Dear, it's been a long time since we had any romance around here."

No matter how you say this, the message your wife hears is, "I'm keeping track, and you're not making it as a loving wife." She knows this as well as you do, and what you have said merely underscores whatever guilt she may be feeling.

On the other hand, you can say, "You know, dear, to me you are more beautiful than the day I married you, and I love you more than ever before. You're terrific; you really turn me on."

Of course I can't guarantee the results of this approach, but chances are it will lead to some "creative dialogue"!

We have the same kind of choice in all our relationships.

When we realize that the people around us are as guilty as we are, and that they don't need their guilt underscored, we can supply the word of affirmation that tells them they are loved, cared for, and appreciated. Husbands need this; wives need it; children need it; even in-laws need it.

Once at a conference I was leading a seminar on the subject of broken relationships. During the final half-hour we had some creative dialogue by opening up the session to questions and answers. The last person to speak was a woman. "Can God heal a broken relationship that isn't just broken—that just doesn't exist?" she asked.

When pressed for an explanation, she said, "My husband and I never quarrel and are never angry. We simply have no relationship. He comes home from work, has dinner, watches television, reads the paper, and then goes to bed."

"Is it like that every night?" I asked.

"Every night for years," she answered.

"Do you love him?"

"Yes," she said, tears beginning to form in her eyes. "I love him very much."

"Do you think he loves you?"

"No, I am sure he doesn't, or he wouldn't be so cold and indifferent."

"Well," I said, "as a Christian, it seems to me that you are the one who must be vulnerable and find out the true nature of your husband's feelings. He must love you or he wouldn't be coming home to this dreadfully boring routine every night. He'd be out bowling or drinking or doing something a little more exciting than what you describe. Perhaps he's hoping that one day something will happen to rekindle the love that you shared when you were first married."

"But what can I do?" the woman asked.

"What are you doing now to try to change the relationship?"

"I keep inviting him to our prayer group," she replied, "and I leave books and pamphlets around, hoping he will read them."

"Is this working?"

"No," she admitted.

"Then why don't you try something much more radical and costly to you?"

"Give me a for instance."

I grabbed at something wild. "Some night when he's watching television, why don't you put on your flimsiest lace nightie and your best perfume, jump into his lap and ruffle his hair and tell him you love him as much as ever. What do you think his response would be?"

"I'd hate to guess," she giggled.

"But what's the worst thing that might happen if you took this step in faith?"

Without a moment's hesitation, she replied, "He might laugh at me."

"That's true. And would that hurt?"

"It would hurt more than anything I can think of."

"This is what faith in Christ is all about, lived out in the dimension of marriage. To leave tracts and pamphlets around and to suggest that your husband come to your prayer group really makes you superior and invulnerable. But to do something like this gives him the chance to respond lovingly or not. Can you take such a risk?"

A few days later, back at my office, I got this letter:

"Dear Bruce, I did what you suggested and guess what? He didn't laugh!"

It was the beginning of a new relationship between the two of them. Of course it might not have turned out well. But apart from something like this radical kind of risking I can see no way in which God can work through us to heal some broken relationships.

No one is more lonely than two Christians living together or working side by side and pretending to be better than they are. Some of the most astonishing miracles I have seen have occurred when Christians have stopped playing games and dared to appropriate the power that God has made available in Christ. Because of this power, they have dared to love each other enough to reveal those things about themselves that could be threatening or damaging.

To illustrate this kind of miracle, let me tell you about the marriage of two people whom I have known intimately for nearly ten years. By varying the circumstances and personalities just a bit, I could make this my own story or that of literally dozens of other people I know. What happened to this couple, John and Alice, is far from an isolated incident. It is typical of those who have heard the good news that in Christ they need no longer be strangers to themselves or to their spouses.

The miracle that happened to John and Alice can be gleaned from reading excerpts from letters they wrote to me shortly after I had spent three days visiting in their home at the time of a conference focused on small groups and the witness of the laity.

First Alice wrote,

> How I wish you were sitting here in my kitchen as you were last Thursday morning. My heart is so full of love and thankfulness that I can scarcely write. If you could see me, you would understand. Except that God spoke through you that morning, you could not have known so clearly what I needed to challenge me to stir me out of my ineffectual spiritual life. I was hungering to grow more fully so that God could use me more effectively to

help others. Somehow I always knew that one day I would have to be honest with John, but I needed a challenge such as you gave me that day.

On Thursday evening, just a couple of hours after you said good-bye to us, I paid the price. The fear I have carried for fifteen years was released in a few minutes as I spoke the truth to John about my past life. I prayed that he would understand, but I never thought the results could be so wonderful. God has blessed me beyond my worthiness with a man who loves me more now in spite of knowing the truth. Truly this has been a miracle of his great concern and love for a penitent sinner such as me.

For the first time in my life I feel like a real, whole person, free of myself, forgiven and accepted by God and by the wonderful man he has given me to love in this life. My love for John has taken on an exciting new depth and meaning such as I've never before experienced. I am free to love him instead of trying to make up to him for my past by pretending; free to admit my failures without fear of losing his love; and even free to disagree with him and lose my temper—which I seldom permitted myself to do before. Free of the need to wear a mask before my family and friends. I feel so released and grateful it is hard to express my joy.

It's been five days since that encounter, and instead of losing this peaceful glow, I sense a deeper presence of Christ in my life each day. I know that days of spiritual dryness will come, but I thank God for graciously granting me this time of complete joy and peace.

On Friday I had an opportunity to speak with a woman who is having a lot of marital discord. For the first time, God gave me love and understanding for this person who has always been so difficult. Although the time wasn't right to speak out completely, I did say enough to shatter her ideas of me with my former holier-than-thou attitudes. What great lengths I used to go to in order to create the impression that "Alice never has any problems, troubles, or temptations!"

Because I had been completely honest with John, a second miracle occurred the following night when we took a long walk under the glory of God's starlit heavens. John was honest with me. Even though his past was not nearly as black as mine, this brought him a release too. He wants to tell you that part himself, one day soon.

The following day I received a letter from John in which he did just that.

As Alice has indicated, on Thursday night we sat side by side in the dark and she told me about her talk with you, her wrestling with the problem previously, and her need to discuss it with me.

What happened before our marriage is of absolutely no consequence to me. As a matter of fact, I did not want to hear the details. I truthfully feel that there was nothing to be gained by her telling it. She was willing; that's the important thing. Maybe this is my weakness—I didn't want to hear!

However, when Alice discussed conditions since our marriage, I was crushed. How it hurt my pride to realize that she had fooled me. I recalled my conversation with you the previous night, when I had complacently stated how happy our marriage was. Truly, I was crestfallen.

My love for Alice was not diminished. I felt fooled, confused, regretful, many mixed emotions, but through it all was the strong threat that I too had something I should confess to her. I admitted this to Alice but could not force myself to do it. I didn't want to hurt her just because she had wounded my pride. We prayed together, asking God's help and thanking him for his blessings and Alice's release.

Next evening we went for a walk and I was compelled to tell Alice about a condition in my life of which I was ashamed, and which has helped cloud the presence of Christ for me. I was somewhat surprised to find that this was not news to Alice; she knows me better than I know myself. But it was good to be able to tell her, good to know that there is nothing we can't talk to each other about.

We look forward to many ups and downs, praising God for the high spots and seeking his guidance during the lows. I pray the lows will be leveled off, but I hope there are always highs such as this last week to show us how gracious our Lord is and how he reaches all of us, even the unworthy ones.

As a friend and confidant of these two and an observer of the witness their life together has been to a great many people, I can say that this experience of theirs has deepened and strengthened over the years. It has lasted.

The dynamics of what happened to John and Alice are clear. Each carried a secret in marriage. Each, out of a misplaced kind of love, was concealing something dark—one in the present and one in the past. When Alice dared to speak out about her secret, John was temporarily crushed, but later able to reveal his secret. At last these two discovered what marriage is all about. The walls came down, and they not only experienced the truth of what they had known before, that God loved them, but also experienced God's love in each other and his acceptance through the incarnation of each other's acceptance.

The same situation can exist between parents and children, if we hide things from one another and grow further and further apart. One of the great miracles of my own life involves my relationship with my older son. For some time this boy had a problem father. I had nagged and criticized and tried to straighten him out because I saw in him an arrogance, smugness, and superiority that I thought needed correcting.

But the more I corrected Peter, the more aloof, withdrawn, and superior he became. Or, at least, so it seemed to me.

Then one day I was working at home and went to Peter's room to look for some paper. In his desk I discovered a poem that he had written:

> Hello out there, world;
> It's me in here.
> Can't you see me?
> What? You're having trouble hearing me?
>
> But I'm in here.
> Yes, that's right.
> Inside where?
> Inside myself, of course.
>
> The outside shell is very thick;
> I'm having trouble getting out.
> Who am I? You say I don't sound like myself?
> That's because you've never heard me.
>
> This other guy? Oh, he's the shell I told you about.
> You say that's me?
> No, I'm in here;
> He's just my protection.
>
> Protection from what?
> From you, the world.
> I can't be hurt here.
> You see, my shell keeps you away.

You, the world, are pain.
I'm safe in here;
I will never be laughed at.
The shell? Oh, he doesn't mind laughter.

Come to think of it,
I'm comfortable in here.
Why should I leave?
Hello, world, still listening?

What's that, world?
I thought for a minute you said something.
It was a faint voice;
It sounded human, real, I thought.
I thought it was answering me.

Maybe not.
I can't hear too well inside this shell.
Well, I feel funny, sleepy,
And it's so comfortable in here, world.[1]

When I finished reading the poem I felt devastated. I realized that the boy I had been trying to subdue and humiliate was really a lonely man, just like his father.

That afternoon when Peter, who was then almost fifteen, came home from school, I told him I had found his poem.

"Did you like it?" he asked.

"I thought it was terrific. Do you mind my reading it?"

"No."

"Peter, I had no idea you were lonely like your father. Forgive me for not hearing and understanding you and relating to you as one lonely man to another."

"But, Dad, you're not lonely. You've got hundreds of friends."

"Well, Pete," I said, "it doesn't matter how many friends one has. There's no escape from loneliness. You wonder what would happen to those friends if the circumstances of your life would change—if you would lose the qualities other people found desirable. Friends are perhaps the greatest thing God can give you, outside of the gift of himself, but even with friends one has deep loneliness. And I suppose the mark of a Christian is that he knows how to deal with his loneliness."

From that point, Peter and I talked about who we are as people. We talked about our needs, and about how Christians ought to be really aware of the loneliness of others in their homes. What struck me in that conversation was the enormity of our sin in being unwilling or unable to hear the silent screams of loneliness from those with whom we live.

Peter, through his poem, was able to reveal something to his father of how he felt. His vulnerability made me less critical for the time being, and able to be vulnerable as well. This was the beginning of a new relationship between two men who not only love each other but who understand their need for each other's love and friendship.

MEMORANDUM

TO: Keith

FROM: Bruce

RE: Chapter 9, Broken Relationships and Moral Failures

Reliving the experience with Peter made me very pensive. I wonder how many people who read this book will be facing broken relationships in their own families the day (or night) they are reading this chapter we're working on.

So many Christians I counsel with appear to believe that making a "total commitment to Christ" or "being filled with the Holy Spirit" will automatically mean that they will not have serious marital squabbles, or that if they do they can merely ask Christ to retake control of their lives and the problems will vanish. When people witness to this sort of simple victorious solving of deep hurts between marriage partners, it triggers a whole set of memories for me of unreal and rosy preconceptions of what the Christian process of coming through a painful marital quarrel is like.

Add something else about this. I know God performs miracles, but I think there are also principles and preconditions involved in this sort of healing which can help give Christ permission to heal us.

B.

❖ I DO NOT EVEN RECALL HOW IT STARTED, but it was bad. We were really mad at each other. I remember estimating to myself that it was probably going to be at least one of those "three-day mads." But there was a hard quality about this time that I did not like at all. We had already been through the open hostility stage. Direct verbal communication had stopped, except for those crisp, necessary exchanges that allow the flow of life with its car pools, etc., to go on. When guests came on Saturday, I remember being amazed to see us responding to them in a perfectly natural way . . . and even to each other in the presence of the guests. After they left, silence dropped again. All Saturday evening and Sunday after church we worked around the yard and house. At meals we spoke through the kids and shot each other down with glances over their heads.

By Sunday night we were both exhausted. I wanted to be alone, but to leave Mary Allen with the children would *prove* I was unreasonable and selfish. Finally, I had a plan. I would suggest that the two of us go to a movie. She does not like to go to movies when she is very tired, so she would refuse, and I could go on alone. But Mary Allen is very perceptive. She said she would like to go to a movie. The theater I suggested was full, so we went to another. This second picture was all about a couple, both of whom did nothing but pick at each other, resent what the other said, and express selfishness. It was a terrible experience; the husband, who was obviously neurotic, even said some of my lines. The show was so revealing that we didn't dare even look at each other. After the movie, we drove home . . . in silence. I realized exactly what had happened to us. I had counseled dozens of couples and had told them what I had found to be a Christian solution for this situation for me. I knew that one of us had to confess our fault in the problem, really mean it, and let the chips fall where they might. You have to sincerely mean it because your mate may well *agree* with your confession and say, "I'm glad you finally saw the problem." But I know of no other way than for one party to somehow see and confess something of his or her responsibility for the problem—even if it is only the resentment resulting from a still unresolved issue.

As we drove along, I considered turning on the radio, but then decided I didn't want to argue—silently—about the music. I saw how bull-headed and self-centered I had been, but I kept reminding myself of *her* part in all this. "Okay," I finally told myself, "you're supposed to be the big Christian counselor. Let's hear you do what you're supposed to do." But when I looked over and cleared my throat, *I could not do it*. "I'll confess later," I thought to myself. But, for the first time in years, I could not. I went to bed filled with resentment. As I lay there in the dark, blinking back tears of rage and frustration, I realized again that I was a helpless little boy who not only could not do what he knew was right, but didn't want to. There was no solution.

The next morning, Monday at 6:30, a dozen of us men met, as we do every Monday morning, to pray together and discuss the experiment of faith in God to which each of us is trying to give his life. This group was made up of anything but a bunch of pious, Sunday school–type fellows. It was almost impossible to be phony with them. Furthermore, not only was there no "victory" for me to report, but there was considerable doubt in my mind regarding any solution to our situation at home. I realized that I really needed their prayers, and that I was just protecting myself and my reputation as a Christian by my silence, since many of them had been honest about the pressing issues in their lives. So I told the group what I have just told you. After a couple of minutes of silence, the man sitting next to me quietly confessed that he had had a remarkably similar weekend. Two other men then related almost identical experiences. We began to talk about our pride and our inability to overcome it. We began to see our wives' side. After we had talked awhile, my whole situation was in some way different. That morning we ended our meeting by praying for each other and anyone else in the world who might be trapped by pride.

When the meeting was over, I couldn't wait to get to the telephone. Now that I *really saw* myself, I was free to call home and tell Mary Allen how I had not been able to get through to her the night before and how sorry I was to put her though all that hell. Although there was some "wind damage" to be cleared up, we both knew that the storm was over. As I hung up, I realized in amazement that *nothing had changed* in our situation since the night before. *Nothing* had been solved. And yet suddenly we were both free to love each other. Not only was I free from the particular situation, but that Monday was the most creative day I had had in months. All kinds of fresh insights about the work I was doing came to me without any straining on my part. In some very important way, as a result of the experience I had just been through, my little world had been unlocked and was available for me to work with. Then I began to understand.

Sunday night I had seen my world, but the people in it were objects who would not bend to my will.

Monday morning, through those men and through our vulnerable sharing of our real humanity with each other and with God, Christ had touched my eyes, and for a day, for a week, I saw the people in my world as I think Christ sees them. Nothing was different—and yet *everything* had changed. I had been looking for days for a plan, a little personal Christian program to undertake, through which my problem would be solved. But God did not give me a plan. He gave me something infinitely more freeing and creative. He gave me a whole new perspective.

As I thought about this experience and many more like it in

my life, I began to suspect that I had been searching in the wrong places for personal renewal in my "Christian life." For years I had been trying every new technique or program I could find that seemed to have value, only to discover that before long each one became a compulsive duty. And finally, many of these "duties" would bore me. I was afraid to admit even to myself that prayer, for instance, sometimes bored me, so I kept searching for new techniques and trying them.

One Sunday evening a few months ago I was sitting with my family when the telephone rang. It was a long-distance call from another state. A young ordained minister whom I had never met was on the line. He had read *The Taste of New Wine*. His wife, who said she had reviewed the book three times, was on an extension. There was a very tired, almost wistful quality in the young man's voice. "What is the meaning of this crazy Christian life, Keith? What's it really all about?" At first I thought that it must be a joke. But in the same instant I realized that it wasn't at all; and as he talked on, I knew what he meant.

"Keith," he could have said, "what happens when a person makes a conscious attempt to commit his entire life to the living God, lives a few joyous, productive years in his church—maybe even becomes an ordained minister—and then wakes up one day and finds that the well has gone dry? 'Faith' becomes only a word again. What kind of a Way is there for people like us—people who have been baptized and confirmed, have practiced the Christian disciplines, and have said all the right formulas after accepting Christ as Savior and Lord? And yet, if we dare to be honest, we are fed up with our *churchy* talking, with the continual religious noise, and with the nervous, seemingly 'manufactured' involvement of our Christian brothers. But still, beneath all our frustration and rebellion, we want deeply to be God's people."

In searching my own experience to try to give them some hope, I began to see that during these past few years God had been giving me a new start, a second touch. As I listened and spoke to this obviously sensitive and committed young couple, I realized that recently I had almost forgotten about "religion"—that instead, I was thinking about people and God and the problems of life, and relations between persons. I remembered that Paul spoke of our having available the gift of "the mind of Christ" (1 Corinthians 2:16). And knowing he did not mean the physical *brains* of Christ, all I could think of was that he was saying that we have available to us the living *perspective* of Christ. Those times when I saw the world through his perspective, although nothing had changed—everything was different. Prayer had meaning again; the Scriptures came alive; and I was drawn out of myself to love other people.

I tried to think of how that perspective has reappeared again and again in my life. Then I remembered that morning with the 6:30 A.M. group and I saw that I needed to try to face my pride sooner and to learn when, where, and how to confess my sins and begin again . . . and again . . . to heal the recurring brokenness in my life with other people. And that this process of facing my pride, confessing my sins, asking forgiveness, and trying to make restitution (when I can without hurting other people) is for me the human groundwork for the miracle of God's healing grace in broken relationships.

CHAPTER TEN

❖

LOSS OF FAITH, FEAR, ANXIETY

MEMORANDUM

TO: Bruce

FROM: Keith

RE: Chapter 10, Loss of Faith, Fear, Anxiety

As I look over my material on broken relationships and moral failures, I realize that I could spend the rest of my life writing and not even touch the anxiety and lostness I feel when I am really separated from the people I love. I suppose I have always repressed some deep childhood fear that everyone would go away and leave me all alone.

Bruce, maybe we had better include some material on trying to handle fear and anxiety as a Christian. This is an area in which "committed Christians" often tell me they feel so guilty for even *having* fearful or anxious thoughts that it's hard to be objective enough to deal with these feelings creatively. They hate to ask about such problems for fear of being "found out in their lack of faith." Are there concrete steps or behaviors new Christians can engage in to deal with their fears and anxieties, besides praying?

K.

❖ Two very different men have taught me a great deal in years past about fear and how to handle it. One was a venerable and highly respected doctor; the other, a professional wrestler.

The doctor, a surgeon, confided that there were only two things in life that he fears—the loss of his skilled hands and a possible impairment of his breathing. Within two years he suffered a double attack: emphysema in his lungs and crippling arthritis in his hands!

Here we see one of the most mysterious and puzzling aspects of fear—its magnetism.

The teenager afraid of unpopularity often ends up a wallflower. The businessman afraid of failure or bankruptcy is likely to have financial difficulty. A possessive mother afraid of losing her children's love and affection will probably experience rejection in painful ways. In the grip of fear, we seem to hasten the approach of the feared object or event.

On the positive side, there is a way to deal with fear that minimizes its power and its effect, and may even turn that fear into an advantage. This is where the wrestler can speak to us.

He stood a magnificent six-foot-nine and was a new Christian, giving his witness with telling effect. When asked how he had happened to become a wrestler, he replied that all through his teenage years he had been a tall, skinny boy with little strength and much fear of physical contact. Then he read a book from which these words jumped off the page: "Do the thing you fear most and the death of fear is certain." He saw the implication at once and began a bodybuilding program that led to his joining a wrestling team.

The Viennese psychiatrist Viktor Frankl says, "The cue to cure is self-commitment." These wise words from the father of logotherapy echo a corresponding spiritual message from the Bible: commit yourself to Christ and do the very thing you fear most.

I would suggest at least six steps to handle fear. Since scientific truth and authentic revelation are apparently never in conflict, and since God is the author of both, we may draw freely from these two sources.

1. Analyze your fear. There are at least two kinds of fear. One kind can be a good friend and a genuine gift of God, but the other is certainly a deadly enemy. Let us label these "healthy fear" and "unhealthy fear."

Healthy fear keeps us from destroying ourselves or others physically, mentally, emotionally, and socially. Children learn fear early in life. They develop a healthy respect for busy streets, hot stoves, and sharp knives. As a small boy I was intrigued by a newfangled cigarette lighter in the car of a friend who came to visit. I was warned never to push it in or to touch it. Well, of course, at the first opportunity I did just that—and for weeks carried a painful circular brand on my thumb. I have been wary of cigarette lighters ever since!

In the adult world an active conscience that tells us when we are morally right or wrong can be a barometer of healthy fear. Fear of consequences often keeps a man honest, moral, true to his convictions, or responsible as a member of his group. A newly emerging school of psychiatry is violently anti-Freudian and declares that a man's conscience is his best friend. It affirms "middle-class Victorian values" that keep a man from becoming a thief or a philanderer. Freud thought that a too-strict conscience caused mental breakdown. The new psychiatry says that mental breakdown comes because we do *not* listen to our conscience and enter into mental conflict as a result, and that when we begin to bring our performance up to acceptable standards, we find mental health.

Generally speaking, healthy fear is based on external threats which are real. To be afraid of real danger is certainly a healthy thing. Unhealthy fear, on the other hand, often appears in the form of anxiety, which springs from inner motivations that may or may not be grounded in reality. We are afraid of rejection, or we are afraid of our own worthlessness, or we are afraid of failing in any one of a thousand ways. This internal anxiety can make all the external aspects of life loom like grotesque giants. To be motivated by inner fears is spiritual myopia. We see life in a distorted way and react in panic.

This is the very opposite of living by faith, which begins when we see things as they really are. This does not eliminate healthy fears, but puts external forces in their true perspective.

So it helps to take an honest look at the things you fear most. Jot them down on a piece of paper and show it to a trusted friend or counselor. Try to discover whether these are healthy or unhealthy fears. Once you have done this, much of the problem may already be solved.

A woman of great faith visited her doctor for an examination. A few days later he told her that she had cancer and that her days were numbered. At first she panicked and fear took over. But in a few moments she regained her perspective and smilingly replied, "Well *your* days are numbered too." She realized that the doctor had not introduced any new evidence. Ironically, the woman outlived her doctor by several years, though he was much younger than she. But the important thing was not her extended life span, but the fact that she lived her remaining years free from fear.

2. *Pay attention to healthy fears.* Often we are in a panic because we are doing something we should not do or neglecting something we should do. This can be the basis for mental breakdown. The old Freudian psychiatry said that because people felt rejected or worthless or full of self-hatred, their performance broke down. The theory was that when your feelings improved, your performance also improved. Clinical evidence seems to indicate that this theory has little validity.

But amazing breakthroughs are coming through the new psychiatry in terms of treatment and cure. Present-day pioneers of the mind such as Glasser, Szasz, Mowrer, and Parker say that feelings *follow* performance. People feel worthless because they are doing poorly. This school of psychiatry tries to help them perform better (to learn to love, to learn to be honest, to learn to be responsible), so that their feelings about themselves will improve. This is certainly not unlike the biblical message calling for repentance. When someone's life is changed, they find that they feel better and that they may genuinely begin to love God and others and even themselves.

3. *Don't fight unhealthy fears.* Viktor Frankl stresses this in homely, simple terms. He says the more you fight an object you fear, the more you increase its hold on you. If you are troubled by insomnia, the worst thing to do is try to sleep. If you are a stutterer, the worst thing you can do is try not to stutter.

Frankl reports great success in helping people with such symptoms. He tells the insomniac to go to bed, saying that he is going to stay awake all night and possibly for many nights. When he makes a game of not sleeping and trying to stay awake, sleep usually comes sooner than expected.

This noted psychiatrist also tells about a bookkeeper who lost his job because his excellent handwriting turned into a scribble. The harder he tried to keep from scribbling, the worse his handwriting became. The doctor told the bookkeeper to begin to scribble as illegibly as he could. When he tried to scribble, he found that he could not, and his former handwriting returned.

Another case involved a boy with a stuttering problem who discovered that when he tried to win sympathy by forcing himself to stutter, he was unable to do so.

Praying to have our fear removed usually avails little. As Christians we should pray instead for courage to launch into action in spite of our fears.

4. Learn to laugh at yourself. When we take ourselves too seriously, we only aggravate our problems and become more difficult to live with. Gordon Allport has said, "The neurotic who learns to laugh at himself may be on the way to self-management, perhaps cure." This advice from a psychologist is profoundly Christian in its implications. The heart of the Christian message is that God loves us and accepts us in spite of recurring fear and failure. We should therefore be able to see ourselves with relaxation and good humor.

5. Risk failure. In biblical terms, live by faith! This is another way of suggesting that we do the very thing we fear most.

The story is told of a shipwreck off the New England coast many years ago. A young member of the Coast Guard rescue crew said, "We can't go out—we'll never get back!" The grizzled old captain replied, "We have to go out! We *don't* have to come back." This kind of living often cuts the sinews of fear.

Christian security at its deepest level has little to do with success or failure. As Christians we believe that Christ loves us totally whether we succeed or fail. This gives us a new base from which to follow God in mission to the world. If we believe that God loves us regardless of our performance, we do not have to hide our failures from ourselves, from our fellowmen, or from God himself. The important thing is that we try to find God's will and do it, and admit when we have missed the mark or failed.

Ultimately we never know whether we have succeeded. The cross looked like dismal defeat, but it became the sign of God's greatest triumph. It may even be said that the will of God for us is not that we accomplish an objective, but that we attempt it. In the case of poverty, for example, we believe it is God's will that we work toward the elimination of poverty, inequality, and ignorance. Whether or not we will ever wholly succeed is irrelevant. I do not believe that God holds us responsible for success, but for obedience. He will judge us by our efforts, not by our successes.

6. *Recognize fear as faith in reverse.* Even unhealthy fear can be an asset to a Christian if it points out to him the focus of his spiritual needs and the particular requirements for faith. When you know your fears, you can almost certainly find God's challenge to you. Do the thing you fear and you may find that you are acting in faith.

A few months ago I attended a great laymen's institute in the Midwest, sponsored by a large denomination. The members were talking about a radical change planned for next year's program. Many people who had been present at this convocation for years were in a panic. Over lunch I turned to one of the leaders and said, "How do you think next year's program will be?" He answered with a smile, "It will be just what we make it." Here we see faith at work. The same situation induced fear in some men and faith in others.

Christians can enjoy the freedom to fail. Many years ago I had to make a momentous decision about my career. For weeks I prayed that God would give me guidance, but no clarity came. During this time I urged my wife to pray for guidance and to confirm what I suspected was God's will.

One day she told me that she would gladly go wherever I went, but that she had no light on this next move. Then I realized that much of my desire for God's guidance was a fear of failure. I wanted my wife's confirmation in the move so that if it ended in failure, we would fail together.

New freedom came when I made the decision with dispatch, not knowing if it was right. My fear of failure in the situation was gone. I came to my new job with enthusiasm and with a great sense of God's love and presence. "Perfect love casts out fear!"

Living by faith does not mean that we will always be right, guided, or successful. Part of the Christian style of life involves a spontaneity in which we lose our fear of failure and move out in the light of the guidance that we have, acknowledging that we may be wrong. It is reassuring to read the Book of Acts and find reports of failure among the first-century Christians. They set up a communal society that failed. They failed to believe in the power of prayer; when they prayed for Peter in prison and the angel let him out, they wouldn't let him into their prayer meeting! They did not understand the unique thing God had initiated among the Gentiles, and for a long time refused to accept them as equals. For years they doubted Saul's conversion. They refused to obey the Lord's command to "go into all the world" and were driven by persecution to do so. They had to appoint deacons to preside at the table because of infighting. Drunkenness, incest, laziness, jealousy, all were found among the Christians. The list of failures goes on and on.

They were far from perfect people, but they had a joy and a dependence on God. They did not seem to hesitate to act for fear that they might be wrong. They believed that God could use even their errors if they were free to admit them and to change their ways.

By nature and also by conditioning, our impulse is always to defend ourselves. Self-defense can take the form of belligerence, silence, ridicule, criticism, or proving that one is right. It all adds up to the same thing: invulnerability. Every natural force in human nature says, "Protect yourself. Don't let people get close to you. Don't let them know your weakness. Don't let them see where you are wrong."

Contrast this picture of natural humankind with the picture God shows us of himself on the cross, when he made himself naked and vulnerable in Jesus Christ.

Vulnerability poses a real problem for many Christians because we have made some false assumptions about what we are called to be and do. Too often we have been under the impression that in becoming Christians we have somehow become like

God: that is, perfect, correct, proper, and beyond criticism. If we fall into this trap I believe we are really missing the Christian style and making ourselves unable to help others.

I see an effective Christian as one who has discovered that God's love is most understandable and easily transmitted at this point of vulnerability. Most of us are drawn to the person who is vulnerable in his relationship with us—who demonstrates that he trusts us. Instinctively, I feel that such a person is full of a new spirit—not a human spirit.

Several years ago in England I met a marvelous woman who served as the lady warden at a lay renewal center. She loved all the people who came there, and believe me, a lot of us were unlovely! Observing how she took time with each guest, I made some assumptions about her. "She really has found the victorious life. She's so naturally loving and saintly. Somehow she is made of different stuff from most of us." I found myself admiring that woman greatly, but by putting her on a pedestal, I somehow created a gulf between us.

Later on that week she was asked to make the evening address. She began by quoting a favorite bit of verse:

> I wish I liked the human race,
> I wish I liked its ugly face.
> I wish when introduced to one
> That I could say, "What jolly fun!"

Through her candid humor and her vulnerable honesty, I saw Christ in her in a new way. Further, it seemed obvious that the unusual love she demonstrates to others is not her own but Christ's. What's more, I told myself, "If it is Christ in her, then this kind of love is possible for me as well." She found it as difficult to love the unlovely as I do. But she did not fear that her lack of love would be discovered. She was vulnerable enough to tell us about it.

MEMORANDUM

TO: Keith

FROM: Bruce

RE: Chapter 10, Loss of Faith, Fear, Anxiety

Boy, we are really just hitting the high spots on these iceberg human problems. I think we ought to do some more on anxiety in the Christian life. People have hit me with questions like: "Is my faith gone when I find that I'm anxious or afraid?" "Does God have a purpose—or at least a way of using anxiety and restlessness *after* one has made a commitment of his life to Christ?"

I guess the main problem I'm hoping you'll take a shot at is the fear that God has "left us" if we get anxious and don't "have faith."

B.

❖ ALMOST FROM THE BEGINNING OF MY INtroduction into the fellowship of Christians, I can remember hearing people imply or say outright that *restlessness, anxiety,* and *incompleteness* were signs of the non-Christian life and that *peace, security,* and *completeness* were signs of the Christian life. When I found out that anxiousness and incompleteness were thought to represent evidences of sin and evil, I started feeling unacceptable any time I was not consciously joyful. Then one day I woke up anxious, afraid, and feeling very insecure—all adding up to a real frightening loneliness and doubt about the reality of my Christian commitment—just when I had seemed to be "getting my Christian life under control."

Thinking that this experience was a sign of evil infiltrating my life, I redoubled my spiritual efforts: more attention to prayers and Scripture reading, etc. And these things helped for a while. But sometimes they did not. Since I felt that anxiety was sinful, I began semiconsciously to have guilt about the anxiousness. This only caused more anxiety. The more I looked within myself, the more withdrawn I became. I did not want to get out and witness about a joyful life when I was miserable inside. Further, I hated to admit it, but my Christian friends began to get on my nerves. They *seemed* so untroubled, and I knew intuitively that some of them *must* have similar problems. So I started faking it again, without even being conscious of it. Someone would call and say, "Hey, buddy, how are you feeling?" And I would reply, "Fine, things couldn't be going better," when in reality I was worried sick. Don't misunderstand, I am not for telling everyone about your every ache and pain in order to be scrupulously honest, but we Christians have begun to feel as if it is a denial of Christ to be miserable. Consequently many of our friends, being human, are left alone and guilty in their times of misery. But I began to see that this position of hiding our humanity is that of the "whitewashed sepulchres," smiling on the outside and rotten with guilt, anxiety, and incompleteness within. I knew all this intellectually, but I caught myself hiding my misery also. My conscious reason was that revealing my feelings of need would harm other people's faith. In retrospect I realize that I was really afraid that people might not think *I* was truly committed, or I wouldn't have these feelings. As I struggled with this problem, I had to take a new look at my humanity—the humanity of a man who wanted with all his heart to be God's person and yet found himself anxious and restless inside. Why would *I* have to have vague feelings of dependency and incompleteness, just when I seemed to be living a disciplined, outgoing life?

In studying psychology and some existentialist literature, I had often read that religion is only a phase, not only historically but in each person's pilgrimage toward maturity and wholeness. In my anxiousness I had the sobering thought that maybe I was about to "outgrow" Christianity, as some of my psychologist friends thought I would . . . or should. I remember being struck particularly by Erich Fromm's conviction that a mature person comes finally to the point of internalizing the idea of God to the extent that he or she no longer speaks of him and he becomes only a symbol.[1] According to this line of reasoning, those of us who continue to *really need God* are only revealing deep dependency needs. The notion these writers present is that hopefully we can outgrow these profound but immature needs, and with them the need for God.

As a Christian, I have often just shaken my head and tried to ignore the troublesome problems these writers suggest. But my own existential anxiety was driving me to take a new look. As I read the Scriptures along with psychological studies on anxiety and dependency, I began to see that Christianity *does* account for these deep needs. People seem to be *born* with a deep disequilibrium and incompleteness (or dependency need) just as physically they are born with built-in recurring hungers for food and sex. It is the activity of these physical needs which forces each child to communicate with the world and shapes the child's relationships and communicating habits. A baby's hunger causes the first scream, and at that moment verbal communication with the world has begun. And I think there are psychological needs as deeply given in the human situation as physical hunger.[2] The deep-seated "dependency" need of which I am speaking is experienced as a vague indefinable restlessness, a need for attention, or for success, or fame, or love—one is not sure what. And this motivating incompleteness keeps us from being *independent* from the rest of the world, so that whatever specific forms it takes, it *is* a deep dependency need. As I indicated earlier, this need drives us from one success or failure to another, from one woman to another, from one philosophy or psychology to another. We are drawn ever onward to different challenges, different people, different spokesmen as we search almost frantically for something or someone to quiet our restlessness.

As Christians, we have realized that this universal existential need is a *built-in* or instinctive need for God and other people, which will not let us rest short of the deep completion and relatedness for which we were made. It was this sense of relatedness I was realizing in my new relationship with Christ and with people around me. At a profound level I knew the *big* search for meaning and security was over, even though I still had uncertain and unsettled times. As Augustine described this universal dependency need in Christian terms: "Thou madest us for Thyself, and our heart is restless, until it repose in Thee."[3]

In wrestling with my anxiousness as a Christian, I saw that this restless desire that drives us to God causes a great deal of our anxiety as human beings. There is a fear that our deepest need will not be met. In fact some people have told me in anguish that they were afraid to *really* commit their lives to God for fear that he would not be real, and *then* what would they do? So they "kept him alive" by keeping their distance, since they could not endure a world without the hope, however remote, that their deepest and most haunting needs would be met. Since the relationship with God and with his people has begun to fill this deepest existential vacuum for millions of men and women, many people in the church have unconsciously assumed that when one truly begins the Christian life, the anxiety should disappear forever. And its presence after conversion is a sign of a relative falling back into an uncommitted state.

But now I was finding that *we do not shuck off this deep need* just because we become Christians. In fact, this drive is the *recurring* hunger that now forces us to *grow* as Christians. When I accepted Christ as Lord and Savior (from the hopeless quest of living without God), this deepest need in my life seemed to be arrested. I felt free from the frantic nature of the basic "drivenness" of life. Having a great purpose now, I set out to live this life through the disciplines, and so on, that seemed to go along with it. But then, when I began to "conquer the disciplines," I started unconsciously not to depend on God and his people but on my acquired knowledge *about* these things. My dependence was once again in my ability, only this time in my religious ability, and not in the strengthening love and power of God. Getting to be known by a few Christians, *I* was being depended on and felt that I must be religious and strong, not anxious and weak—when the truth is that I often am anxious and weak. But I had subtly put myself in God's place again, to be for other people that which they needed—God. But he is the only One who can meet our basic dependency needs. He designed them. And I had become anxious and incomplete again because I had conquered the techniques and was unconsciously on the hunt once more for a deeper security than they provided. At last this search sent me to my knees as a child, beginning again. It was my anxious sense of incompleteness which God had used to drive me back to the place where I would again put my life in his hands. For me then, Christian restlessness was not *necessarily* bad, but, like physical pain, it could be a warning signal—warning me that something was overloaded in my life, that something was out of balance. And because of the signal which anxiety provided, I could stop and do something before I destroyed myself.

When I realized that our existential sense of dependency and periodic anxious restlessness are a part of the fabric of Christian living, I was quietly awed. Instead of driving me away from Christianity, as this discovery has some of my "God is dead" (or seriously wounded) friends, I was thrilled. Because this discovery—that my restlessness is there to get my attention and point me back toward Christ—freed me as I had never been freed *to be human* as a Christian. If my faith is in God, then my job is not to build a successful, untainted religious life; it is to live a joyous and creative human life. I am to love him, love his people, and love living, as poor and incomplete as I am or ever will be—yet free not to have to be a God-shaped wooden saint. My recurring restlessness is a natural part of life, driving me ever deeper in my relationship with him. I found that the more my ultimate trust was in God, the *less* I tended to be involved in *neurotic* dependency relationships with people. And I saw how Jesus could live trustingly among people but not lay the burden of his *primary* trust on them, knowing they could not fulfill it (John 2:24). And in some way which I could not understand, the more ultimately I was dependent on God and not ashamed to be weak, the more power I seemed to have to help people.

At about the time I was wrestling with this matter of inner

weakness, I remember being asked to speak to a men's group on the subject "The Christian Life." I went to the meeting and spent five or ten minutes telling the men very honestly that I was feeling miserable. I was tired of speaking to groups and of being a Christian, and had even considered not coming that night. Then I told them what I had thought about my life that day. I had realized that whatever else had had meaning to me besides Christ was so far back in second place that I had decided to come and tell them that I was a Christian almost by default. I had come to the meeting on the chance that some of them might live with misery and incompleteness too—that some of them might be looking for a Way that could give purpose and meaning even to restlessness and its accompanying despair in themselves. I had thought that my honest and specific confession of my miserable restlessness and self-centeredness would force these men to reject me and any message I might have to give them. Instead, I found a room full of brothers, of warm, struggling fellow human beings, who also needed a second touch from their Lord, even though many had been committed Christian ministers for years.

As I thought about the power of that experience of simply being human with those men, yet a professing Christian, I took a look at the New Testament. I saw that Paul had some very anxious, despairing moments, being "so utterly, unbearably crushed that [he] despaired of life itself" (2 Corinthians 1:8). J. B. Phillips, the New Testament translator, in discussing this matter points out the fact that as Christians "we can be overcome by the most terrifying darkness and reduced to a sense of inadequacy amounting to near desperation."[4] He goes on to say that "the stiff upper lip business is not necessarily Christian; it sounds much more like a throwback to the Stoics than to early Christianity. . . . The letters [of Paul] tell no story of idealized human beings but reflect the life of people who are changed but by no means perfect."[5] I was understanding, finally, that the burden of being happy for Christ was not mine. I was free to own my true feelings on any given day—without denying Christ.

Some people in the church today are talking about a "totally committed" state in which one is forever delivered from restlessness or anxiety. But when I talk with such people or when I read about the life of "total and continual peace" in a devotional book, I try to see what the author's *life situation* was like. In a number of cases the totally trouble-free Christian person, although perhaps resigned to material poverty, has in some way been insulated psychologically from any future severe change in his or her material responsibility in the world. Some have joined monastic orders, some have flung themselves on the world "to let God provide." This latter course may seem to require the greatest kind of courage, and in many cases it may; but having tried it in one sense, I have found it also *can be* a real abdication from responsibility. As to security, I have never heard of such a person starving in our society. Some "totally peaceful" Christians have had enough materially from secure jobs and are content to keep these jobs and minister in them. Some have been housewives who have had good providers. I am grateful that people can be freed to live for Christ, unencumbered by the threat of the competitive material world. I think, as a Christian, one might— within the walls of such a situation—avoid existential anxiety and restlessness, perhaps almost indefinitely in some cases. But when one becomes *genuinely psychologically vulnerable* in the world, I believe he or she *will* have anxious moments. I do not think these anxious moments are evil or that they necessarily indicate a lack of Christian courage. As a matter of fact, if one is *not* afraid in truly threatening circumstances, then Christian courage is a mockery.

We get the idea that to be courageous is to be totally unafraid and not anxious in the face of real danger. Most fear is a natural reflex action to a genuine threat to one's life or well-being. Healthy people have it. It goes along with the instinct of self-preservation. Anyone who is not conscious of any fear in a genuinely threatening situation is seldom heroic. Instead, he or she is more likely to be grossly insensitive or out of touch with reality. I have come to believe that Christian courage consists in *seeing the danger fully*, reacting to it with human finitude and fear, and *yet* being willing to face the dangerous situation for Christ or for a brother or sister, with God's support. God did not say he would take us out of the humanness of the world. He said that he loves us and will be with us and that through faith we can overcome that human weakness and can act with courage *in spite of* it. So, although we still experience fear, God has given us a "cure" for it—an overriding trust in the love of God.[6] Paradoxically, it is the experience of fear and restlessness which brings back a recurrence of the personal realization of one's humanness, and a new commitment encounter with the living God, at increasingly deeper and more subtle levels of awareness about life.

Many psychologists have found that recurring times of human restlessness seem to cluster around certain crises or stages in every person's life cycle. Erik Erikson has postulated eight stages of development which represent distinct crises in life.[7] If this is true, then there are certain times in the life of everyone (Christian or not) when the very threat of moving into a new phase of living makes that person again terribly vulnerable and anxious, and yet these circumstances have nothing necessarily to do with sin or evil in his or her life. Although this is relatively current thinking in the psychological world, it has been interesting to note that the church realized the gravity of most of these same basic crises *over a thousand years ago* and set up sacramental means to help the believer face most of the same transitions within the loving and strengthening context of the body of believers.[8]

My own experience and investigation have led me to believe that committing my life as wholly as I can to God and receiving the reassuring sense of his Spirit does give me a deep and ultimate security my humanity has longed for. But, when and if one discovers that he or she is *again* anxious as a Christian, that person can know that Christ counted on his disciples having troubled hearts and told them he was sending the Holy Spirit to comfort or "strengthen" them when they did (see John 14). So I have come to see that restlessness and ultimate dependency, like pain and evil, are woven into the fabric of life and that Christ does not abolish these for the Christian, but periodically they may become the motive power to drive us toward fulfillment in him. *

Understanding this, however, has not changed the fact that I find it very unpleasant to be restless or discouraged. It is all very well to understand that God will teach me something from these inexplicable and anxious times and bring me closer to himself, but they make me very lonely and it is quite another thing for me to find a practical way out of them. I have discovered that these periods often lead to long and unproductive sessions of introspection and discouragement.

---

* I am here talking about periodic bouts with restlessness leading to anxiety about one's spiritual health. If, on the other hand, the Christian (or anyone else) is continually anxious or afraid, I would suggest that he or she go to a qualified counselor. Many of our anxieties have physical and psychological roots and can be alleviated through counseling.

CHAPTER ELEVEN

❖

A STRATEGY FOR HANDLING FAILURE

MEMORANDUM

TO: Bruce

FROM: Keith

RE: Chapter 11, A Strategy for Handling Failure

Sorry I ended Chapter 10 on a "discouraging note" in saying I sometimes get snarled up trying to handle some of these problems. But it's true. The paradox is that they don't scare me as they did, and I know now that there is a way through them by which I'll grow and learn more about God and life. This paradox—failing and changing or growing through the process—seems to me to be one of the often unnoticed recurring themes in the Bible and the Christian life.

When we enter a relationship with God, how much change or improvement can we expect? Since we all seem to fail and are filled with different kinds and degrees of guilt about it, how do we deal with that guilt and failure?

Please include a "little dab" on that one.

K.

❖ ONE OF THE GREAT MARKS OF A RIGHT relationship to God, it seems to me, is that I can begin to talk to God as the man that I am at the moment and not as the man I would like to be or as the man that I think God would like me to be. It means that I begin to believe the incredible love of God, and thus honor him by affirming that love through my own openness and trust and honesty.

A friend of mine taught me a great lesson one morning as we were having a cup of coffee together and getting ready to face the tasks of the day. We try to "check in" with each other as often as possible, to listen to each other and to share whatever concerns are on our minds. That particular morning when I asked my friend how he was doing, he said, "Terrible. I had a fight with my wife last night and we went to bed not speaking to each other, sleeping back to back. But this morning she gave me a kiss and said, 'Honey, I love you.' "

"What did you say?" I asked eagerly.

"I said, 'Well, I don't love you and I don't love myself and I don't love God. I can't think of anybody that I do love. But I'll tell you this: I'm going to pray this morning and I believe that sometime in the near future God will straighten me out because he loves me. He will make me able to love again. And when he does, I promise to put you first on the list!'"

This kind of honesty frees us of the need to pretend and allows us to be ourselves before God and before people. It affirms our trust in a God who will not only forgive but will also change us into the kinds of people he would like us to be and that we ourselves would like to be.

Isn't this the dynamic behind David, the Old Testament king and psalmist? David was a man whom God called "a man after my own heart." But he was not a good man, and if he were alive today, I doubt that he could get the endorsement of a pulpit nominating committee or the credentials to enter a theological seminary. Among other things, David was a thief, an adulterer, and a murderer. Nevertheless, he was a man after God's own heart. To understand this is to plumb the depths of God's love for humanity.

When David saw his sins, he admitted them before God and others and made no defense for himself. But he went beyond mere confession. He believed he was forgiven even though he was a sinner.

There is a marvelous scene in the Bible describing David's behavior when he had rediscovered again the amazing grace of God. He danced before the Ark in the sight of all the people of Israel. His wife Michal shouted at him, "Come in; you're making a fool of yourself." Not only was David dancing, but he was wearing some sort of kilt or short skirt and apparently he had no underpants on. Michal, the daughter of a king, was outraged and humiliated.

"I can't stop!" David shouted back, continuing to dance wildly before the Ark, celebrating the good news that God forgives and justifies sinners. Having confessed openly his own unrighteousness, David was free to celebrate the grace of God.

How many of us confuse the good news of God with "religion" and have wasted our time and destroyed ourselves and others by having to maintain some kind of righteous stance? I believe the gospel is for those who understand that they are not righteous and who can claim the gift that God offers: his forgiveness and cleansing and unconditional love.

The direct connection between our relationship with God and our relationship with others is affirmed and reaffirmed countless times in Scripture. John said, "How can you love God, whom you have not seen, if you cannot love your brother whom you have seen?"

To love is to trust, and to trust is to reveal those things about yourself that could give someone else the weapons with which to hurt you. Until we can be this vulnerable we cannot truly love. And it is not enough to be vulnerable to God; we must also be vulnerable to other people.

One of the greatest Christians I know has been for many years the head of the world's largest conservative faith mission. Norman is an Englishman and one of God's unique and delightful saints. He tells about the time, years after his conversion, when he was in East Africa with the Christians in Uganda during their great revival. In their vulnerable style of life he saw a contrast to his own pretensions. One night after being with these Christians who believe in "walking in the light," as the phrase from John's first epistle has it, Norman went back to his hut and got on his knees and began to confess to God his sins against his wife, who was still in England. He began to confess his shortness of temper and his irritability.

In the midst of this confession to God, he suddenly heard the still, small voice say, "Norman, don't tell me. *I told you.* Go and tell your wife."*

This is why confession must be not only from ourselves to God but between ourselves and other people. It is God himself who reveals where we are missing the mark. To tell him about our sins is simply to acknowledge that we have heard what he has been telling us. The real test comes when we can let go of our righteousness and tell at least one other human being about this new insight that God has given us regarding our disobedience or unfaithfulness.

---

* Sometimes because of the nature of the sin (e.g., involving a third party, etc.) or the unstable emotional condition of the one sinned against, you may have to seek out a pastor or a Christian brother or sister with whom you can confess to God.

We speak about the Christian style as one of both vulnerability and affirmation. In our relationship to God we realize that the Good News is not our response to a doctrine or a theology, but a response to a person. The gospel is embodied in a person affirming us: Jesus Christ saying, "I love you unconditionally. Will you give me your life?"

We cannot respond to this with "true" or "false" any more than we can respond to the statement, "I love you. Will you marry me?" by saying "true" or "false." We can only say yes or no. To say yes is to return affirmation with affirmation. We affirm God by yielding to him, even as he has affirmed us by giving us himself in the person of Jesus Christ.

A true, affirmative commitment to Jesus Christ may be as simple and prosaic as this: "Well, Lord, I love you, and here is my life. I've changed what I can, but there are certain things I can't change. I have certain assets and liabilities that are a part of my birthright and training. I've got some sins of my own making. Some of them I'm stuck with. And Lord, I can't promise that I'll be good. I want to be good, but I can't promise that I will be. But here I am. I give myself to you. Do with me what you will."

When we enter into a right relationship with God, just how much change or improvement can we expect? In one sense we never change. The new creation that God has promised us if we accept Jesus Christ begins as he starts to deal with some of our inner conditions that do not change. For example, if we are full of guilt, it can help us to discover grace. If we are full of fear and give it to God, our very fear becomes faith. Our loneliness, transformed by God, can help us to love. Criticalness can become discernment. Phoniness or hypocrisy, when confessed to God and others, can become freedom.

Grace, faith, love, discernment, and freedom are all, therefore, the "products" of inner conditions given to God—but the inner conditions do not disappear. We have a choice of living with these inner conditions, unacknowledged, unsurrendered, and uncommitted to God. Or we can give all these qualities into God's keeping and see them transformed.

It is much like the case of an alcoholic who joins AA. He never ceases to be an alcoholic, but by the power of God he can live free of alcohol and he can become a part of God's creative purpose in setting other alcoholics free. Nevertheless, all the while he is a part of this process, discovering sobriety and sharing his newfound strength with others, he reminds himself publicly and privately that he is still an alcoholic. This crucial point in the AA program has made it unpalatable to some doctors and psychologists and also to some alcoholics who have managed to find sobriety in other ways; yet I believe it to be realistic and in large part responsible for the success of AA in helping defeated people.

Again we are reminded of King David. A sinner and a rebel, he could nonetheless face his faults and stand in God's presence, celebrating the Good News that he was loved, forgiven, cleansed, and capable of transformation. And I think it would change the church profoundly if we Christians could be like this.

The Old Testament provides us with another character study that gives the other side of the coin. In the ancient poetic drama of Job, we find revealed the tragic example of a good man who missed this central message of God's grace.

Job is a good man—far better than David. With all his problems and plagues, the death of his children and the loss of his property, and finally the terrible illness that besets him, Job is able to keep trusting God. But when his so-called comforters try to find the flaw in Job's nature that made God punish him so cruelly, Job defends himself and declares that there is nothing in his nature deserving of punishment.

Job's self-defense was his problem. He was a good man who

missed the point; King David was a bad man who did not have to justify God or defend himself.

Perhaps this is the radical nature of the Christian style which we should learn to demonstrate for the world. The Christian is not always right, always virtuous, or always guided. Not at all. He or she is often wrong, errs frequently, and makes many wrong turns. But a Christian is someone who does not have to defend or justify himself or herself—and has been freed by the grace of God from the need to be someone or something other than himself or herself.

Martin Luther said that a Christian ought to love God and sin boldly. Does this sound shocking? It should not, for Luther believed that all human endeavors and activities are tinged with sin: that no one is capable of complete unselfishness.

However, there is another sense in which we might take Luther's advice. To me it means that the Christian, wherever he or she lives or in whatever century, ought to be adventuring and trying new things, totally unafraid of failure. We live in a world where failure is always at hand, and where guilt is bound to rise up at every turn to plague us. Take, for example, a man who has been working late night after night for a long time. One evening he says to his wife, "Tomorrow, dear, I will be home early. Let's plan to go out for dinner. You and I are going to celebrate."

But the next day as he is about to leave his place of work, a man for whom he has been concerned comes in to say, "I need you right now. I am in desperate trouble."

Our friend is then faced with a choice of whether to fail his wife and stay with the man in need, or fail the man and go home to a promised date with his wife. Whatever he chooses to do, he cannot be sure that it is right. Guidance may not come instantly.

The mark of an authentic Christian is that if he decides to stay and help his colleague, when he goes home hours later to a furious wife, he does not justify himself. Rather, he says, "Honey,

I prayed, and I did what I thought was right. But perhaps I was wrong. Please forgive me."

It seems to me impossible for a Christian to live so cautiously and circumspectly that he never gets into a situation like this. When one is totally and vulnerably involved in the needs of people, conflicts are bound to arise and people are bound to be hurt. The man who tries desperately to avoid conflict, to avoid sin, is really saying to the world that he is afraid that God cannot or will not forgive, that God's grace is not sufficient.

The true person of God, like David, can move out into creative relationships and adventure, implying that he or she may and will fail. But when that happens, the failure is not justified by blaming God's guidance.

It is a matter of desperate importance that Christians understand the unavoidability of guilt. We are not people who, because we are Christians, cease to be guilty; we are not always guided or spirit-filled. Rather, we are people who no longer have to pretend that we are the innocent party in dozens of relationships and situations day by day.

There was a real turning point in my life when I came to a new understanding of the nature and meaning of public worship. I belong to a denomination that holds communion to be tremendously holy and sacred, and for this reason in our tradition we have communion four times a year, or at most, once a month. It is always an occasion of great solemnity, with special effects accompanying it, both by the choir and by the elders who serve.

Therefore, I had been bothered for years by the matter-of-factness with which Roman Catholics and Episcopalians seem to regard communion. The sacrament is administered every Sunday, and communicants come forward to receive it as casually as if they were coming forward to accept a cup of tea. At least this is how it appeared to me.

Then one Sunday I was worshiping in the Episcopal church in my hometown, and when the invitation was given to come forward for communion, the theology behind this tradition, which provides the sacrament often and in a matter-of-fact way, suddenly made sense to me.

Here were people who had inherited a centuries-old tradition—a tradition which understands that human beings are rebellious, sinful creatures who generate enough guilt every week to destroy themselves. What can we do with this kind of guilt? We cannot sing it away, or study it away, or erase it with good works, or even pray it away. There is only one means I know by which we can deal with this wrongness in life: we can confess it and receive the grace of God which is sacramentally remembered in the elements of bread and wine.

This matter-of-factness represented a much more profound understanding of the nature of human beings and the nature of God and the celebration of Good News than did my own tradition, which makes the occasion so special and solemn.

Without accepting God's love and forgiveness day by day and week by week, we will surely be swamped by the bilge water that seeps through the leaky hulls of our lives. At least once a week we can honestly face ourselves and honestly deal with God's offer to forgive and cleanse. This is the source of the Christian's joy and celebration. It is not that he or she is no longer guilty, but that we have accepted God's answer for our guilt and gladly celebrate and bear witness to that answer.

MEMORANDUM

TO: Keith

FROM: Bruce

RE: Chapter 11, A Strategy for Handling Failure

I feel like I talked around in circles some on that one. But it's always been hard for me to articulate some of these things which came through the "sweat, blood, and tears" route of learning. My own sweat sometimes fogs my spiritual lenses.

What do you do when you are down and trying to come out from under your own guilt and failure and the loneliness and despair you've told me you get into?

B.

❖ THE ONLY "WAY OUT," I HAVE FOUND, OF the sort of loneliness and despair that result from my long periods of self-centered introspection is this: a simple style of life that I resist. I resist it because it seems too insignificant to change my condition, because it appears to be too much trouble and does not seem to involve important enough issues to fulfill my anxious needs for relatedness at such times. I also resist this way out because it might lead to rejection.

The process of discouragement in my life seems to work something like this: When I can't complete something on which I am working, when I become afraid about health or the future, or when things get sort of "dry" or I get anxious—when these things start happening, I begin withdrawing into my soul and looking within in order to find out how to get back to happiness and be God's person. I start imagining disaster—everything from financial failure to my wife's infidelity or my children's possible unhappiness in life. But then, before I know it, I find that I am bogged down in self-pity and hopelessness, searching frantically for "peace" and "direction" and a way back to faith. As the situation gets to be unsolvable, the search gets more and more urgent.

Again and again, I find that God brings me out of these pits by a simple yet seemingly impossible route. I finally get so sick of myself and of trying to see the blueprint for the next twenty years that I have to put down my spiritual binoculars and quit my frantic scanning of the horizons of my consciousness. Finally, alone and exhausted with my self-absorption, I may sit and cry and admit that I am lost, bogged down, and wrapped up in myself. I can truly see that "there is no health in me." As I confess these conditions, I can often look back and realize that only in God have I known hope in my own past. Then, at last, I give up. I give up my self-diagnosis and my frantic efforts to avoid failure, either physically, psychologically, or materially. And I give up my dreams for success. I give them to him, finally being willing to have them fulfilled or not. And strangely, this is like dying, to give up these dreams of success in any venture, since my whole destiny seems to be riding on them. Then, since I have given up the "big" plans for my life (like trying to be an outstanding psychologist, writer, or success in business), I am interested only in sanity for today.* Paradoxically, it is at this point that I am ready to live again. Since I have quit sweating something unreal—the results of my life *tomorrow*, I am free to begin working with the building materials which are real—the hours in *today*. I begin to slowly wipe away the tears and blink in the morning light of a new day and to notice individuals immediately around me again. I begin to see the shapes of trees and flowers and hear the sounds of birds singing and fussing at each other, and children shouting and dogs barking, and the vastness of the sky—all of which have been going on "out there" but which have been sealed off from the inner, windowless sweatbox in which I do my serious worrying about myself.

It is impossible to describe what may then take place, except it is at this point somewhere that healing often begins for me. And strangely, I have to take the step of beginning again as an act of faith, since I do not *feel* like acting at all. It's just that I finally get so sick of going over and over my own situation until I could scream, "There's no solution for me!" . . . that I turn back to God. And when I can get beyond my compulsive desire to "solve it all myself," I may be able to give up the sweatbox. To walk out

---

* Or sometimes if I am afraid of something, I have to stop and say to myself, "Yes, this thing I fear *could* happen to me—even the threat of death. But God would be there; and with him as my audience I could start again to face the eventualities this event would bring about." And sometimes this very *acceptance* of the possibility makes the specter lose the sharpness of its horror.

of it is a real act of faith since I get the feeling at such times that I *must* attend to the outcome of my problems or they will never get solved. But the truth seems to be that I am like my little girl who was continually picking the scab off a wound to see if it had healed. There is a sense in which I reach a point at which I have looked at my situation until any more direct attention to it, even in prayer, becomes a step away from Christ. I have to walk away in raw faith believing that God will work beneath the scab.

About this time in the process, some morning I wake up and *see* my wife again. I begin to concentrate on what is going on *with her*. I start forcing myself to listen carefully to the children at breakfast again. I start to ask questions to find out if I really know what they are saying and to let them know that I understand, when I do.

On such mornings as I start out to work, I begin to see people as individuals, persons with homes and families and needs. In short, I begin to live "in the now." At such times I often feel dead to happiness and optimism. Sometimes I am only keeping on for another hour—knowing numbly that this process of keeping on for Christ is the thread of faith which must lead to his will. And since no other process seems to help, I find myself at such times "keeping on keeping on," partly out of obedience to Christ and partly out of a deep intuitive knowledge that, as painful and paradoxical as it is, personal suffering is a real and important part of the human way Jesus came to show us. J. B. Phillips was a real help to me in commenting that today we seem to "assume that we have a 'right' to be happy, a 'right' to live without pain, and somehow shielded from the ills which flesh is heir to. Evidently the early Christians thought no such thing. They quite plainly took it as an honor to suffer for Christ's sake, and here (in the New Testament) the advice is to accept all kinds of troubles, whether they are apparently for Christ's sake or not, as friends instead of resenting them as intruders."[1]

As I have begun in these moments to try to crawl out of the slough of self toward Christ and others, I have realized that at least I can use my miserable days for him by trying to love his people and do his will. Also, I have found that there is a strange dilation of the soul's eyes in "keeping on" through one's suffering for Christ's sake. My own misery often sensitizes me to the signs of lonely agony in other lives which I would have missed otherwise. Besides these things, John Coburn speaks of the positive acceptance of one's own suffering as a way of participating in a very real power God releases into the world, a power which allows other people to be strengthened to embrace and carry their own burdens as they see us carrying ours.[2] This trying to do God's will, this increased sensitivity to others, and this possible release of power into the world—these things at least give periods of anguish some meaning. And through all this I have discovered what Viktor Frankl meant when he said that "suffering ceases to be suffering in some way the moment it finds a meaning."[3]

As I have forced myself to begin again in faith to live once more in little ways, often before I know it, I have felt the faint stirring of a fresh breeze through a life which a day before had been stifled by self-pity and oppressive loneliness. What I often find happening on those days when I begin to reach out to people around me in personal ways—oh, such little ways—honestly listening, really watching, is that I may become for that day truly a Christlike person, a caring man. And since I have then started filling my thoughts and prayers with real people and events instead of specters and imagined disasters, my prayer life and Scripture reading deal less with the hypothetical and more with real life. And whatever may happen to my future, I have the feeling at the end of such days of having lived as an authentic human being, reaching out toward others as Christ did. At such times I have understood how close Camus came unconsciously to describing true Christian living when he had his hero say thoughtfully, "Heroism and sanctity don't really appeal to me, I imagine. What interests me is being a man."[4] Because the longer I am on this crazy Christian pilgrimage, the less I want a static condition called "sainthood"—or rather the more I believe that to *be* a saint is simply to be a person in the ordinary world, but to be *Christ's* person. It seems more and more apparent to me that to be a living child of God is to be a working apprentice to a fantastically careful Artist in the field of creating and sustaining life, freedom, and relatedness out of the clay pits of loneliness and despair all around us, this day.

It is impossible to overstate what this simple change of focus has meant to me in terms of social contacts and relationships in my daily living. In the competitive milieu in which I have been raised, I have only had time for people who "count," people whose destinies were linked to mine in terms of social status or interests and general economic desires. But I am finding in this new perspective that people who might not have counted in any of the old ways can be interesting and can be subjects for my involved attention as *important* people in themselves, because they are important to God.

These friendships are much more natural and deeper because they are based on the sharing of the loneliness and hopes which are the very foundation blocks of our common humanity. Such friendships do not have to be pumped up by the compressed air of frenzied, score-keeping social functions. And the great dawning insight of this perspective to me is that if the ordinary, "unimportant" people in the world become interesting and fun to be with, and if even loneliness and discouragement have value in learning to live for Christ—then *any place*, any job or vocation or marriage can be a place of fulfillment and potential happiness. I saw in retrospect that for so long it was much too important to be with *the* sharpest people in sight. When I wasn't with "them," I felt restless and not fulfilled somehow. But through the changing of the focus of my attention, God is opening the doorway to the world of his people, the people along the paths I am walking today who fear, hate, suffer, and hope and who are waiting for Love to come and fill their lives.

And what happens to me as I bring up from the almost dry well of my own life a few small cups of water for people around me and begin to pay attention to them and love them? I sometimes find, after a day, a week, a month, that the anxiety and hollow dryness are gone. While I have been looking the other way into people's lives, I have again been made new by participating in God's love.

❖

CHAPTER TWELVE

A STRATEGY FOR FINDING YOUR DIRECTION— YOUR PROMISED LAND

MEMORANDUM

TO: Bruce

FROM: Keith

RE: Chapter 12, A Strategy for Finding Your
Direction—Your Promised Land

Reading back through these chapters makes me excited and
sad, excited because I can see how many ways God has made
life more real and given *everything* in it more meaning, even
difficulties and failures. But I'm sad that I don't have more
help to give other people who want to try this adventure. Yet I
suppose God has to bring each of us along his or her own set
of hills and valleys in order to teach us to live with our particular set of problems and gifts. And maybe all we can do for
each other is to witness to the fact that there are things like
hope, grace, forgiveness, and innumerable new chances for
travelers on the journey.

Maybe we ought to close the book with some material on
the nature and direction of the adventure itself. What is the
call to commitment, Bruce?

K.

❖ THE INITIAL CALL TO DISCIPLESHIP WAS A call to adventure. The early disciples were called to leave their families and the comfort and security of familiar ways and places, to go they knew not where, and to do they knew not what. Day by day they discovered that life was a great adventure, and that every hardship and every setback was a doorway to new service and maturity. Christ's call to his people, then and now, goes far beyond perfecting us, polishing us, or making us adequate. I see it as a call to follow him into a life of involvement with people and into situations that formerly would have threatened us.

I once asked a charming and dynamic Christian woman in Alabama what was the biggest change that Christ had made in her. She replied that for the first thirty years of her life she had been haunted by a fear of failure. She had turned down all kinds of jobs and opportunities lest she fail. Yet today she is so filled with "holy boldness" that it is difficult to imagine her fearful of anything. This is the kind of change that Christ can bring about in his disciples.

Responding to the call does not always mean success in the world's terms. Two men I know, a plumbing contractor and a stockbroker, went bankrupt shortly after responding to Christ's call. But for each, "failure" led to a much wider ministry and a much deeper experience of life and service.

Recently I had lunch with a man who owns a chain of restaurants. He understands his particular call in terms of seeing his business as his parish, and all the people working for him as his spiritual and economic responsibility under God. He has become a person who is able to listen deeply to others, to ask questions, and to pray expectantly. Over lunch he recounted miracles in the lives of some of his employees who were "problem people" only a few weeks before. A new kind of teamwork is developing in the heart of his flourishing business.

Some months ago my wife and I were doing a television show in a large Eastern city. The announcer for the telecast had responded to the call of Christ some time before. He and his wife, partners in a mixed marriage and the victims of much misunderstanding, were reconciled as a result of their Christian commitment. But the most impressive thing to me was the number of people in that studio who had begun the Christian life or who had become intrigued by it because of the simple, dynamic love in this man. He was not an "evangelist," but simply an announcer living under new management, whose life was contagious to those around him. Surely this is the Great Adventure of our time for all us Christians, in our families, neighborhoods, jobs, and schools.

A couple in our town in New Jersey has meant much to my wife and me over the past years. George is a businessman and Florence an attractive, vivacious homemaker. Someone asked them, "What would you do if you knew you couldn't fail?" They talked about a ministry to lay leadership, and how much they would like to attempt such a ministry. After twenty years in the same business, George has left his job. He and his wife are now engaged in the ministry they had envisioned, and God is doing marvelous things through them.

A man on the West Coast once told me that his preschool son had asked his mother, "Mommy, are we live or on tape?" This is a question that we should ask one another in the church. Is life spontaneous or simply a dull, repetitive routine? The Good News is that Jesus Christ is calling all who will hear to follow him. The call is to a commitment to him as Savior, to his lordship over us, a commitment to fellowship with one another, and a commitment to adventure in every relationship and situation.

MEMORANDUM

TO: Keith

FROM: Bruce

RE: Chapter 12, A Strategy for Finding Your
Direction—Your Promised Land

In this last section I mentioned several people who found
that their commitment to Christ led them to a change in their
vocational life. How would someone know if he should leave
his job (or stay) for Christ's sake if he began to feel that he was
in the wrong place? How would a Christian go about deciding
what the "right" job for him or her might be? Since you've
moved seventeen times in twenty-five years, do you have any
guidelines on how to decide where to go? And if one can't find
a new place, how can that Christian learn to be Christ's person in the place in which he or she must stay?

B.

❖ In the first place many people find that once they have tried to commit their entire lives to God, including family, job, and success, their perspective changes so much they see that many things which were "unbearable" about these different areas of life are not such important problems after all. Many "problems" in a marriage or a job are anxiety-provoking because of the threat they pose to our ultimate security and happiness. For instance, if a man is being teased or talked about by a fellow employee, the threat of losing his job or of not "being considered a man" may make the job almost unbearable. But when one realizes that he is accepted by God just as he is as a person of worth and value, then he may not be so threatened and may not respond in such a way that he triggers the teasing behavior. And then his job may seem right to him.

What if you feel, as a result of your commitment to God, that you are in the wrong job? I've found it helpful to check the possibilities of change in the following manner. First, you might list, as they come to you, all the things you'd like to do (if money were no consideration). Let your imagination go freely. You may have always wanted to be a cowboy, a bank robber, a coach, a ski instructor, a movie actress, an insurance agent, a model, or a dancer. List the first ten things which come to mind *regardless of how* impractical they may sound.

Then go back and eliminate all the choices you can. For instance, if you are a Christian you could probably eliminate bank robber. But any choices you cannot definitely eliminate for moral reasons you may be able to start investigating by writing a few letters or making some phone calls. This is sort of like rattling door handles to see if you can find a door that is unlocked. Every time you are able to *close* a door for sure, say a prayer of "thanksgiving." Usually people get discouraged when they find a door closed, but every time you prove something is *not* feasible you are getting more into the world of real choices and out of an unreal fantasy life.

You may eventually get your choices down to two or three possibilities. *Then* you have a real choice available as to whether or not you can risk a change of vocation.

Then you can take a piece of paper for each choice and list all the reasons you would like to do each thing and perhaps the reasons against each choice. You may find after a lot of investigation that all you can do realistically is what you're already doing. Then you can concentrate on being God's minister right where you are.

Several years ago a man had come a thousand miles to a layman's conference I was also attending. In a counseling interview he told me that he was at his wit's end. For six years—ever since he had become a Christian—he had been in turmoil about whether or not he should go to seminary and become a pastor or stay in a family-owned business in which he was doing very well.

As we talked it turned out that he enjoyed his work except that he was continually frustrated and worried about whether he ought to go to seminary.

After about an hour I told him something I couldn't remember having ever said to a person in trouble: "I think I can solve your problem." He was amazed and overjoyed. "How?" he asked. I asked him if he had a telephone credit card. He did. I inquired about his grades in college, etc.; then a call to the seminary revealed that with his grades there was no way he could be accepted as a divinity student at that school. He said that was the only place he'd want to go to. I said, "Okay, if that's the way you really feel, then your problem is solved. Go home and continue being God's man in business." He did, and several years later wrote and told me how happy he was as a businessman trying to witness to his Lord. But he could have saved himself six years of misery by some commonsense checking of his possible alternatives.

Most of us, it seems, will be faced with the same job or vocational situation, at least for a while, after we become Christians. If this is to be the case, then how can one change his vocational place into the scene of his ministry for Christ?

What If You Stay Where You Are?

When I made the personal discovery that for me, God is real, I was all alone on a roadside. As a matter of fact, it was four years after trying to commit my whole future to God before I ever heard or gave a personal testimony as such. All I knew was that something had happened to me which convinced me that God was performing a revolution in my life. My attention was focused in a new direction and for the first time as an adult, I felt at home in his world. For a while, this was enough.

But soon I began to feel that my own new commitment to God was different from those of the minister and many of the leaders in our church, although I could not explain the difference I felt. I began subtly rejecting them by my questioning and doubting as to the depth of their understanding of the Christian life. Not knowing anyone who seemed to understand what had happened to me, I lived alone inside. I began by trial and error to build a life of prayer, study of the Scriptures and of devotional books. Not having the advantages of a community of people to tell me what to expect as a new Christian, I had to look and decide for myself how a man might live in the contemporary world, trying to be Christ's person. Those first years were lonely and discouraging in many ways, as I tried to learn to live all over again. I had no group with whom I could test what I was discovering.

Then, some four years later, I met an old friend who had also (much to his surprise) been converted. But he had been confronted as a part of a group, and many of his friends' lives had begun to change at the same time in the same church. I cannot tell you how thrilled I was not to be alone with my new faith. It wasn't long, however, until I realized that my open expressions (of anxiety, for instance) made some of those Christians uneasy. I learned that, without seeming to realize it, a number of these people had received Christianity as a sort of "package deal." There seemed to be an unpublished list of things which made one more and more acceptable as a Christian. I was a little baffled and felt that there was something unreal about the idea of continual "unbroken joy" in the midst of vulnerable living. I had not seen this kind of "tensionless peace" in the lives of Christ, Paul, Augustine, or any of the other spiritual companions of my previous four years. Nevertheless, since these new friends were obviously filled with love of God, and since there were many of them and only one of me, I tried to conform. And I knew a great deal of happiness and release in trying to live for Christ. Yet, as much as I loved these Christians and as much as they taught me, I found that I was lonely and restless inside. I felt that no one understood me; and having a desperate need for approval, I was pretty miserable.

One morning I awoke and said in my prayers, "God, I have cut off all my audiences—the old oil business bunch, the folks we party with, the vestry of the church, and now this new group of Christians. I don't fit anywhere. No one really appreciates the struggles I seem to have."

Then, out of the silence, it was as if God said to me, "*I* understand what you are going through. Why don't you play your life to *Me* as your audience? I'll give you the personal consciousness of the acceptance and love you need for your life right where you live and work."

What a simple thought this appears to be as I write it. Yet, when it really hit me, this idea became a profound turning point for me in trying to live as a Christian—in a world which didn't particularly care whether or not I did. At first I did not understand how deeply this consciously "playing it to God" could change my life—until I was having a conversation with a friend of ours who was a college football coach. This man's teams had the longest winning streak in the nation. To watch his boys play was sheer joy. They were in superb physical condition, but what impressed me most was their great drive, their motivation to play every minute as if it were the final minute of the game. In practice sessions I remember having the distinct impression that if the coach might say he wanted six players to tackle a Greyhound bus, *eight* would have raced to be first. This, I reflected, was not the sort of motivation we had at our church.

Since I was then wrestling with the problem of how to get people motivated to become involved in the church's program, as well as how I might live for Christ, I went to this friend and asked him to tell me his philosophy concerning football, and I took notes. He told me some fascinating things—that football is basically a "spiritual" game in that the winner between two teams with nearly equal physical ability is determined by an inner quality of desire to give oneself *totally*. Although this desire is a corporate thing, it must also be deeply individual. I listened to see if I could find out how an individual player on this team might maintain this motivation week after week under the terrific pressure of a long winning streak.

As our conversations continued, I began to see something I had not noticed at first about the players' performance during games. One of the devices the coach employed regularly was the use of game movies for training purposes. On Monday the whole squad, including the coaches, would come in and go over the movies, seeing the good and the bad plays. In talking to some of the players, I had realized the almost fanatical sense of loyalty and respect many of these boys had for their coach. As I watched the replay of some of the films, I saw that these boys did not seem to be playing the game primarily to the audience in the grandstand. They had a reputation for jumping up after being tackled, running back into the huddle, snapping out, and hitting hard with another play. When the excitement of the game mounted and the crowd grew frantic (the other team often becoming rattled), these boys worked like parts of a well-oiled machine. One day as I watched a game, I understood how this could be. Although the crowd might not know if each boy executed his specific assignment well, the coach would know. Their cool operation would be seen on Monday even if the press had missed it. I thought, *these boys are unconsciously playing the game to a different audience and it has freed them from the franticness of the crowd!*

I had my answer. Whether or not it was true for the football team, it was true for *me!* All of my life I had been influenced too much by the moods of my associates. When they were excited and panicked, I reflected their anxiety. Now, in my new experiment, although I was still performing in the same circles and in the same social and business "games," I was occasionally finding a calmness and an ability to live with more honesty and integrity than before. I was starting to play my life to a different audience—to the Living Christ.

I wasn't thinking in terms of his "judging" my actions—but rather of his living *awareness* of my struggles to be his boy. I began to get up in the morning being conscious of God's awareness of me and my waking movements. I began being able to tell him that *he* was the one for whom I wanted to perform the day's actions. Just the conscious act of deciding *that* was a new kind of commitment which, by itself, changed all kinds of things.

Language, for instance. The way I have talked has always depended, to an amazing degree, on the people to whom I was talking and those within hearing range. There was a semiconscious editing for the sharpest persons in the group, even with regard to the tone of my voice. If I found myself in a business deal with someone from the deep South, for instance, I might go home with a subtle and unconsciously acquired Southern accent which only Mary Allen would notice. The men I might be with also affected my *style* of relating to people. For example, if I were to invite someone whom I respected tremendously to spend the night in our home and to walk through an entire day with me, it would improve my conduct without *any conscious discipline* on my part. While this important person was in our home, I would be a little bit more pleasant about correcting my children (and my wife). I would probably be more attentive to the people who waited on me at the post office or bank.

In retrospect, I realized that I have often been just a little more *Christian* when there was an "important" Christian with me. And, in this same way, as I consciously attempted to play out my days and hours before a present, attentive Lord, I began to change with regard to my specific consideration of other people. I caught myself saying silently things like, "Look at this guy, Lord, he needs you. Help me to know how to love him for you." This was a private inner process of disciplining myself to cultivate a consciousness of Christ's nearness in every conceivable situation. And this "concrete" awareness brought about all kinds of subtle changes in my reactions to people and circumstances.

Being conscious of Christ's attention not only affected what I did and said, but what I *saw*. And just seeing people differently changed entire relationships. There was one man, whom I disliked intensely, whose office was close to ours. He was arrogant and a smart aleck; he needled people viciously, many of whom, like the secretaries, could only choke back tears of embarrassment and anger. This man was mad at the world. As an angry smart aleck (which is what I saw when I looked at him), he had no use for Christ's love. But as I began to look at this man, being aware that Christ and I were looking at him together, I began to see—in the same person—a man who was deeply hurt, threatened, and *very* lonely. This is what this man really was inside. It dawned on me that for a man like *that*, Christ's love could have meaning. When I responded naturally to what I now saw as I looked at this man, he began to drop the façade of anger, and the hurt began to come out. Suddenly we were at ease with each other *without anything having been said* to break down the wall. Just by trying to look from Christ's perspective, I saw the real person behind his mask, and somehow he knew and felt loved. I was seeing why the saints had come up with such seemingly simple, basic ways to relate. It was not because they were brilliant. Most of them were not. They had a different perspective; and from that spiritual vantage point, they looked at the unsolvable problems other men saw. However, they saw—in the same situations—different problems. They saw problems which *could* be dealt with through the love and acceptance of God. They saw men as Christ saw them.

I had always vaguely believed that God loved and understood me. But now I was beginning to grasp the notion that God was aware of me and giving me the personal approval I needed to risk changing my attitudes and behavior. The image of him, giving me his attention and understanding at each point in my day as I tried hesitantly to be his person, gave me great support. This "practicing the Presence" took a lot of discipline and effort, and I failed pitifully. I would start out in the morning and forget "to play it to God" before I got the car started! But each time I realized that I had shut him out, or each time that I really fouled up and did it my way, I would stop and confess that I loved me more than him. And I would start again *right then*.

But as I usually am, I was terribly impatient. I kept looking for "results" every day, even though I knew that the lives of the saints have attested that the *real* results are seldom visible to the pilgrim himself. As a matter of fact, instead of saintly results, I began to see the many ways in which my habitual behaviors were *not* God's ways. I wanted to change everything right now! In my impatience, I was like the man in Bruner's story who planted a new onion and pulled it up every morning to see if it was growing. I became very discouraged, and then I met the Reverend Ernest Southcott from Leeds, England. I was an intense young Christian and my urgency for changing the church *today* must have been written across my forehead. After an hour or so of conversation late one night, he asked me, "Have you ever considered *tunneling*?"

Tunneling! I was not sure what he meant, but I did not like the sound of it. When you tunnel, you disappear. I was more of the "cliff-hanging" type of Christian, clambering up the sheer slate cliff, in my imagination, as I risked failure to find a way over the mountainous obstacles of the faith—shouting back down to my more timid brethren, "This way; it's all right!" or "Watch out for the sliding rocks here," as I tried to find a path over the treacherous new ground of our generation's attempt to be God's people. It was as if God were telling me through this man, "If you ever did make it over the mountain, anyone would have to be a spiritual athlete to follow you; but if you begin now to dig a tunnel, even the crippled ones could make their way."

Southcott had said that he had tunneled quietly in his parish for five years, trying to learn how to live his faith and to work as a minister, before he had "seen" any results.[1] Somehow his life told me intuitively that he was right.

I sat down and said to myself: "I will not look for any results for five years, but will make my life an experiment played out to God alone. I will try to immerse myself and my 'actions in relationship' in the perspective of Christ, trying to move into his spiritual vantage point through study, prayer, and involvement with other people."

What relative freedom! I had never realized that it is the *results* of my actions which have always made me afraid. I had been under pressure to succeed as a provider, parent, husband, and Christian because of the semiconscious fear that the results of my actions would somehow not be enough. I never knew when I had done or given what I was "supposed to." This compulsive doing, because of unseen guilt and insecurity, had come out in some strange ways in my Christian life. For instance, I remember when I had finally developed a regular fifteen-minute quiet time of prayer in the mornings. Then, one night at a meeting, I heard a man speak who said he could not get along without thirty minutes of prayer a day. I wondered secretly if I was praying "enough" and if I should pray more—and compulsively did so.

But after my talk with Ernest Southcott, I was being freed from comparing myself with other Christians' "results." This released me more often to concentrate on the details *of the tasks and relationships before me,* instead of on how I was doing as a Christian. I realized that all my life I had unknowingly let other people's abilities and experiences intimidate me and cause me to feel that I was failing.

I remember teaching our little girls to ride a bicycle. Each one wailed through teary blue eyes, "Daddy, I'll *never* be able to do it. Look, the other girls can ride with no hands." I told them to "forget about the other kids and just learn to ride with me holding you." And one day each one would realize that I was no longer holding tightly, and they would have learned. It seemed to me that God was telling me, "I'll look after the ultimate effectiveness of your life. You just learn to go through *today* . . . with Me holding on . . . and forget about the results and what the other Christians are accomplishing in their lives." By agreeing not to take my spiritual temperature each day, I quit thinking so much in terms of doing "religious" things and began to relax a little and live. And in consciously opening my inner stream of awareness and allowing Christ to be the traveling audience to the unfolding drama of my insignificant days and nights, they no longer seem to be insignificant.

It is difficult to describe the intimate sense of discovery I felt in beginning to notice small things around me. The world was filled with surprising sights I had always seen, yet never noticed before. If the little ordinary relationships in life could provide the raw materials for meaning, purpose, and creative fulfillment, then I was beginning to be infinitely wealthy. My life could always be potentially full and growing, whatever my "success" in the eyes of the world might be. It was strangely exhilarating—as if I were standing on the edge of an intimate and lifelong adventure with Christ.

Note: For information regarding a thirteen-week group-study course, *The Edge of Adventure: An Experiment of Faith,* write to Villa Publishing Company, P.O. Box 26744, Austin, Texas 78755-0744.

SOURCE NOTES

Chapter 1: Life Before a Christian Commitment

1. William Temple, *Readings in St. John's Gospel* (London: Macmillan, 1963 [1st ed. 1939]), p. 24.
2. Paul Tillich, *The Shaking of the Foundations* (London: S.C.M. Press, 1949), p. 151.
3. Andrew M. Greeley, *The Jesus Myth* (New York: Doubleday, 1971).
4. Viktor Frankl, *Man's Search for Meaning* (New York: Beacon Press, 1964), p. 163.
5. Paul Tournier, *The Meaning of Persons* (New York: Harper & Row, 1957), p. 135.
6. Thomas Gordon, *Group-Centered Leadership* (Boston: Houghton Mifflin Company, 1955), p. 83.
7. William James, *The Varieties of Religious Experience* (New York: Random House, Modern Library, 1929 [1st ed. 1902]), p. 205.

8. John Knox, *Life in Christ Jesus* (New York: Seabury Press, 1966), p. 84.

9. O. H. Mowrer, "Sin: the Lesser of Two Evils," *The American Psychologist* 15 (May 1960):301.

Chapter 2: Taking the Gamble—Commitment

1. Dietrich Bonhoeffer, *The Cost of Discipleship* (New York: The Macmillan Company, 1960 [1st ed. 1949]), p. 53.

2. Martin E. Marty, *A Short History of Christianity* (New York: World Publishing Co., 1962 [1st ed. 1959]).

3. John R. Stott, *Basic Christianity*, 8th ed. (Grand Rapids, Mich.: Wm. B. Eerdmans Pub. Co., 1962), p. 130.

4. John Knox, *Life in Christ Jesus* (New York: Seabury Press, 1966), p. 87.

5. Thomas à Kempis, *The Imitation of Christ* (London: Collins, 1957), p. 253.

6. Hannah W. Smith, *The Christian's Secret of a Happy Life* (Old Tappan, N.J.: Fleming H. Revell Co., 1968), p. 39.

7. Frederick Buechner, *The Magnificent Defeat* (New York: Seabury Press, 1966), p. 42.

Chapter 3: Conscious Contact With God—Prayer

1. Martin Buber, *I and Thou* (New York: Charles Scribner's Sons, 1958), p. 110.

2. *Ibid.*

3. See Jolande Jacobi's *The Psychology of C. G. Jung* (New Haven: Yale University Press, 1962), chapter 1, p. 5 f.

4. Martin Luther, *Works*, v. 36, p. 86.

5. Louis Fischer, *Gandhi, His Life and Message for the World* (New York: Mentor Books, 1960), p. 34.

6. *Ibid.* See Christian expressions of this experience reflected in the fourteenth chapter of Romans.

Chapter 5: Relationship Pressures and Changes Because of Contact With God

1. Erich Fromm, *The Art of Loving* (New York: Bantam Books, 1963), p. 108 f.

Chapter 7: Job, School, and Neighborhood

1. Alfred North Whitehead, *Adventures of Ideas* (New York: Mentor Books, 1933), p. 286.
2. Karl Barth, *Deliverance to the Captives* (New York: Harper & Bros., 1961).
3. Dietrich Bonhoeffer, *The Cost of Discipleship* (New York: The Macmillan Co., 1961), p. 32.

Chapter 8: The Church

1. This analogy adapted from that used by Donald Snygg and Arthur W. Combs in *Individual Behavior: A New Frame of Reference for Psychology* (New York: Harper & Bros., 1949).

Chapter 9: Broken Relationships and Moral Failures

1. "Hello, World" by Peter Larson, © 1969, Faith at Work, Inc.

Chapter 10: Loss of Faith, Fear, Anxiety

1. Erich Fromm, *The Art of Loving* (New York: Bantam Books, 1963). See Chapter II, especially pp. 53–69.
2. For a brief discussion of one group's experimental attempts to understand "exploratory behavior" [man's motivation from within to search for knowledge about life] see Daniel E. Berlyne, "Curiosity and Exploration," *Science*, 1966 (July 1), Vol. 153, pp. 25–33.
3. *The Confessions of Augustine* (New York: E. P. Dutton and Co., Inc., 1951), p. 1.

4. J. B. Phillips, *The King of Truth* (New York: The Macmillan Company, 1967), p. 64.
5. *Ibid.*, p. 65.
6. See *The Life and Letters of Father Andrew*, ed. Kathleen E. Burne (London: A. R. Mowbray Co., Ltd., 1961), p. 252.
7. Erik H. Erikson's "Eight Stages of Man," *Childhood and Society* (New York: Norton, 1950), pp. 219–33.
8. Note the similarity of Erikson's eight stages to the seven sacraments as historically recognized in the church. See *The Book of Common Prayer* (1953 ed.), p. 607, for list.

Chapter 11: A Strategy for Handling Failure

1. J. B. Phillips, *The King of Truth* (New York: The Macmillan Co., 1967), p. 70.
2. John B. Coburn, *Prayer and Personal Religion* (Philadelphia: Westminster Press, 1957). See chapter on "Suffering and Joy," p. 90 f.
3. Viktor Frankl, *Man's Search for Meaning* (New York: Beacon Press, 1964), p. 179.
4. Albert Camus, *The Plague* (New York: Alfred A. Knopf, 1948), p. 231.

Chapter 12: A Strategy for Finding Your Direction—Your Promised Land

1. See *The Parish Comes Alive* by Ernest W. Southcott (New York: Morehouse Gorham Co., 1956).

ACKNOWLEDGMENTS

We express appreciation to the following publishers for permission to reprint and, where necessary, adapt copyrighted material in this book:

ZONDERVAN PUBLISHING HOUSE for material from Bruce Larson, *Dare to Live Now* © 1965; Bruce Larson, *Living on the Growing Edge* © 1968; Bruce Larson, *Setting Men Free* © 1967. Used by permission.

WORD BOOKS for material from Bruce Larson, *No Longer Strangers* © 1971; Keith Miller, *A Second Touch* © 1967; Keith Miller, *The Becomers* © 1973; Keith Miller, *The Taste of New Wine* © 1965. Used by permission.

	PAGES IN THIS BOOK	PAGES IN ORIGINAL SOURCE
Chapter 1	15–21	Larson, *Dare to Live Now*, 11–16.
	21–22	Larson, *Setting Men Free*, 98–101.
	24–33	Miller, *The Becomers*, 113–125.

Chapter 2	36–38	Larson, *Dare to Live Now*, 63–65.
	38–39	Larson, *Living on the Growing Edge*, 51–52.
	39–40	Larson, *Setting Men Free*, 105–106.
	40–41	Larson, *No Longer Strangers*, 64–65.
	43–52	Miller, *The Taste of New Wine*, 23–33.
	54–58	Miller, *The Becomers*, 53–57.
Chapter 3	61–73	Miller, *The Taste of New Wine*, 53–67.
	75–79	Larson, *Dare to Live Now*, 67–72.
Chapter 4	82–100	(All new material)
Chapter 5	103–114	Miller, *A Second Touch*, 57–64, 83–88.
	115–123	Larson, *Dare to Live Now*, 27–34.
	123–125	Larson, *Setting Men Free*, 69–71.
	125–129	Larson, *Dare to Live Now*, 45–50.
Chapter 6	132–142	Miller, *The Taste of New Wine*, 37–49.
	144–148	Larson, *Dare to Live Now*, 57–61.
	148–150	Larson, *Living on the Growing Edge*, 28–32.
Chapter 7	152–157	Larson, *Dare to Live Now*, 51–56.
	157–160	Larson, *No Longer Strangers*, 119–22.
	160	Larson, *Dare to Live Now*, 56.

I Miller, Keith &
Mil Larson, Bruce
The Edge of
Adventure